THE CLEAVERS DON'T LIVE HERE ANYMORE

THE CLEAVERS DON'T LIVE HERE ANYMORE

PAULA RINEHART

MOODY PRESS
CHICAGO

To Stacy,
who shared this book with me

About the Author

Paula Rinehart entered the Christian scene during the sixties herself, where she followed the trail of great expectations and big dreams that have so characterized those in the postwar generation. She knows firsthand what this generation thinks, feels, welcomes, rejects—why they have experienced a crisis of faith, a deep sense of abandonment, and a load of false guilt, and how they can deal with their struggles. Through her writing and speaking, she has helped others deal with their own struggles of growth and midlife transition.

A former acquisitions editor with NavPress, she is the author or coauthor of four previous books, including the 100,000-copy best-seller *Choices: Finding God's Way in Dating, Sex, Singleness, and Marriage,* which was named Campus Life's Book of the Year in 1984, and *Perfect Every Time: When Doing It All Leaves You with Nothing.*

Paula and her husband, Stacy, have served on the staff of the Navigators for more than fifteen years. They make their home in Raleigh, North Carolina.

Contents

Behold, I lay in Zion a choice
stone, a precious corner stone,
And he who believes in Him shall
not be disappointed.

1 Peter 2:6 (NASB)

Preface

When I began this book, I could not begin to envision the note on which it would end. More accurately, I was afraid of the note on which it would end.

I realized that during many of the months I was writing I was in a tunnel some would call midlife. And I had no assurance that it was possible to come out on the other side—renewed and better for the wear. All I could see then was a disillusionment that threatened to leave me jaded, and, for all I knew, maybe grays and browns and blacks were all that one could hope for to paint the second half of life. Maybe from here on you just grunted your way to the grave.

In the midst of that, I experienced some of the wild, crazy urges for which midlife is famous. I thought about learning to hang glide or scuba dive, but my children said they wanted to grow up with their first mother. I counted at least three cosmetic surgeries by which I could profit, though doctor's offices leave me cold. In the end, however, I decided to face the issues in front of me head-on.

When, after many ups and downs, ins and outs, I began to emerge from that dark tunnel, once again seeing the world in living color, I could not have been more surprised. *To what do I attribute this new turn in the road?* I wondered. *A change of diet? A recent trip overseas? A special act of grace?*

I finally realized it was the actual process of writing on the topic that was causing my inner metamorphosis, for as I wrote, I spent hours skimming the cream of nearly fifty conversations with men and women at similar places in their own lives. Little threads of their stories and experiences encouraged me. Their lives mirrored back to me feelings and conclusions that were mine as well. *I've felt that way, too. I just never had a word for it,* was my inner response over and over. For their stories—and in many cases, for their friendship—I owe them more than I can say.

To list all their names would be difficult, but I want to mention a few. To Tony and Becky Metcalf, Marnie Haden, and Maureen Rank: I am grateful for your willingness to let me share in a wide range of your experiences and insights. To Melissa Hammock, Paul Borthwick, Karen D'Arrezzo, Russ Johnston, Brent Curtis, Marty Russell, Ralph Ennis, Bill Barnett, Dave Mayfield, Mike Bellah, Meredith Gandy, Alice Lawhead, Walter Byrd, Jim Duncan, Traci Mullins, Bob Nielson, and Billy Grammar: A special thanks as well for your stories and the candid, refreshing way you opened your lives to me.

I have often felt overwhelmed by the task of trying to write from a perspective that reflects some aspect of a whole generation. Undoubtedly, others see our journey differently. Writing on a topic like this is like being a referee in a high school football game—you can only call the play from your particular vantage point.

Nevertheless, I want to acknowledge the help of others who have stood at different points on the field than I and who have shared with me their viewpoints. I am particularly thankful to Jim Dethmer, Dr. John Hannah, George Barna, Jack Skeen, Dr. Jim Engel, Jack Simms, Dan Hays, Dan Allender, William Willemon, Josh McDowell,

Dr. J. P. Moreland, Roger Randall, and Fran Sciacca. I am also grateful to Sue Monk Kidd and Calvin Miller, two individuals with special sensitivity and perceptiveness in the arena of life passages. My special thanks to my editor, William D. Watkins, for his patient encouragement in this process.

In the same regard, I would be remiss if I did not acknowledge others who have written more extensively about life stages. The works of Daniel Levinson, Gail Sheehy, Cheryl Merser, and William Bridges, in particular, have influenced my understanding.

Throughout this book, I have purposefully omitted the names of individuals except for the three whose stories are followed in detail, lest the reader lose track of who said what and whose story is whose. The names of these three individuals have been changed, but they represent real and living people, with some details altered to preserve their anonymity. I have spent so much time trafficking through their lives in the past two years that they feel like family. My respect and admiration only grows for the way they have confronted their own struggles and disappointments.

It is for all these reasons that writing this book has been a gift to me. My experience has been enriched by the people I have known, by friends who have shared their lives with me. This book brought me to a deep, genuine sense of gratitude that wells up in me as strongly as the disillusionment ever did.

It is a God-given place, one where I can catch my breath. I stand here encouraged, less aware of what I've lost because I realize I've been given much more in the process.

PART 1

THE GENESIS OF BIG DREAMS

I wanted to do something no one had ever done before. I wanted my life to be extraordinary.

Jim Roberts, 45

1
An Invitation

There was a moment, one in particular, when I first felt older-than-young. The evidence that I was getting older had been plain enough, to be sure. I could look in the mirror and point out a few gray hairs, and I knew from the growing assortment of moisturizing creams, wrinkle concealers, and styling gels that it was taking more time and trouble to look good these days. But I still thought of myself as a woman who at least bordered on the young side until the day a man almost my age changed my perception.

Dressed in gym shorts and solid white Nikes, I was jogging at a perfectly respectable pace on the Y's indoor track during lunch hour. In fact, I was moving faster than many of the crowd. But out of the corner of my eye, I could see a man gaining on me, and in a few seconds he was squeezing past. I stepped aside to give him room. As he slipped by, he lowered his head and said graciously, "Thank you, ma'am."

Ma'am, I said to myself. *Of all the nerve!* I fought the urge to run ahead and ask him if he realized that this was the South and *ma'am* is a term of deference reserved for older women—much older women. "Ma'am is for your mother and your maiden aunt," I wanted to say.

Instead, I watched him at a distance. His hair was thinning in the same places mine was peppering with gray. He was no spring chicken himself and certainly in no position to call me "ma'am." I thought about getting a closer look when a voice in my head restrained me. "You're not eighteen anymore," it said. "You're thirty-eight. Maybe it is starting to show."

In struck me at that moment that maybe, just maybe, I had crossed over into middle age.

I am not alone. At least forty million people are presently making their way through a passage known as "midlife." We are part of a famous group of Americans born after World War II, between 1945 and 1964. Over the years we have been given many labels: War Babies, the Pepsi generation, the rock generation, the me generation. We have had many names, but the label used most often is baby boomers. I shrink from using that phrase, yet that is what we are.

We have been studied and scrutinized, celebrated and lamented, everything but ignored. Ten years ago the editor of *People* magazine, Landon Jones, wrote a landmark biography of our generations called *Great Expectations: America and the Baby Boom Generation*. Because there were so many of us heading into the tumultuous middle years of life, he predicted that our culture would soon be immersed in the throes of midlife on a mass scale.[1]

Indeed, a few years later, Michael Nichols, the director of a large outpatient psychiatric clinic, began to write about the large number of "profoundly troubled" thirty-five- to forty-five-year-olds who came in for treatment, struggling basically with their transition from youth to middle age. The rise of stress and anxiety in our generation indicates that we are indeed having difficulty adjusting our dreams to reality. Like time-release capsules all going off at the same time, we are confronting in earnest the issues that make up this notorious passage in life.

Midlife is no picnic for anyone, for any generation. It

can be a trying time filled with questions, confusion, and an internal scorecard of losses. A host of ambivalent feelings accompany the questions, *What's missing here? Why can't I finally get what I want? What do I want, anyway?* The ideals of youth crash head-on into some of the hard, immovable barriers of real life. It's no wonder midlife is often the infamous harbinger of anxiety and disappointment

But there are two reasons the passage through the middle years promises to be even more challenging for those of us born in the twenty-year span following World War II. The first relates to our place in this century. The prosperous "good time" decades of the '50s and '60s, when we grew up, led us to expect a great deal out of life and, consequently, to greater disappointment later.

We were wonder children, born in wonder years with all the advantages and opportunities our parents could bring our way. *Scarcity* and *hardship*—those words belonged to a generation that had grown up through the Great Depression and World War II. Our generation was beyond that. These were the good times, the good life, and we were invited to claim our share. The world was our stage, and we found out too late that not everyone would get to be a star. That was the foundation of our great expectations, one explanation for why we now find life to be more problem-plagued, more overwhelming than we ever dreamed.

The second reason relates to the renaissance of interest in Christianity in our age group during the '60s and much of the '70s. The years 1966–72 are increasingly regarded as marking a "mini-revival" among youth.[2] The Jesus Movement and the explosion of campus parachurch groups, such as Campus Crusade, the Navigators, and InterVarsity, gained tremendous momentum. Josh McDowell, who has spoken on college and high school campuses for more than twenty-five years, said he has never seen equaled the degree of enthusiasm and spiritual interest he saw among youth during those six to ten years.

That spiritual awakening, with its accompanying effervescence and idealism, coincided with our formative years. Authors William Straus and Neil Howe, in their book *Generations: The History of America's Future 1584–2069*, conclude that our generation is one of five in American history that qualify for the label "idealist": the Puritans (1584–1614); those of the Great Awakening (1701–1723); the Transcendentalists (1792–1821); and those of the Missionary Alliance (1860–1882).

In our case, idealism led us to establish unconscious connections between our expectations of life—which were big enough—and our faith in God. Thus from two avenues, one cultural and the other religious, we have the makings of a more turbulent, disillusioning passage through our middle years than any other generation in this century.

Something Feels Wrong

The first hints of "something amiss" tend to sneak up on people at different ages and circumstances. For me, the critical birthday was between the two most notable ones, thirty and forty. Though I concealed my misgivings well, the year I turned thirty-five was pivotal. I felt as if the rug had been pulled out from under me. I was someone who had been standing on a street corner, waiting for a bus, which I suddenly realized was never going to come.

I was face to face with the unwelcome realization that my life showed every evidence of working out much differently than I had pictured. Without realizing it, I had forecast a time in my life when I would feel as if I had finally arrived. I would have career moving full speed ahead, overachieving children, close friends, an attentive husband, a well-decorated home—or some litany like that.

I had never formally laid out all my hopes. I only knew that there was a great disparity between the kind of life I had dreamed of and the kind of life I had. I was shaken.

It was not that my life was noticeably unpleasant. I lived in a house on a quiet street with books in every corner and plants in the windows, with a husband and two children, a dog and a station wagon. My life was nothing if not ordinary, and that was much of the problem. It was ordinary, middle-aged, predictable—and disappointing. The excitement and wanderlust, that take-on-the-world enthusiasm of my earlier days was missing, and I didn't know where it had gone. I was left peeking out from behind a stack of bills and unironed shirts.

One day I unearthed an old cardboard box that contained some of the memorabilia of my college days in the late '60s and early '70s. I was struck by the scarcity of sorority party favors and other standard college trinkets. Instead I thumbed through dog-eared sermon notes and faded blue booklets that communicated the basic message of Christianity in four concise points. Brochures for weekend conferences and snapshots of old friends with their bags packed stared back at me. I found my first Bible, the *New American Standard Version* I had chosen on my own. It was still wrapped in "Blueprint for Revolution" paper. I had to smile. What had become of the young college girl who had eagerly scribbled the notes in its margins?

As I contemplated the contents of the old box I realized that I was looking at the markings of my own spiritual journey, the transcendent place where I first looked beyond my own life to find an anchor of meaning, purpose, and identity. I was looking at the genesis of my understanding of life and God and faith, and what I might expect from all three.

Undoubtedly, there was some connection between my present gnawing sense of personal disappointment and the spiritual dreams that lay embodied in that box.

Where Do You Fit?

There's a man our age in the White House now. Fleetwood Mac, a little older and a little grayer, played for his inauguration. The civil rights revolution, the struggle over women's rights, the battle over abortion—those were our issues—and we have brought them with us into center stage.

The reality that we are old enough to be and feel like adults in charge of something important begs a good number of personal questions. They are the questions that anyone asks in the middle of life. What have I done with my talents, my time, my life? Have I made the right choices? What have I lost along the way? What can I regain?

Dante seems to be the first person to record his similar struggle:

> Midway through life's journey I was made aware
> That I had strayed into a dark forest,
> And the right path appeared not anywhere.

Dante was thirty-five years old in 1300 when he wrote those words and frustrated because his drive for a political position had been thwarted. Sound familiar? This thing of watching your dreams evaporate—even change shape drastically—is difficult and painful in any day and age.

For people born into the good times that followed World War II and raised on the curds of whey of the spiritual idealism that followed that process is even harder. We have more to contend with—bigger dreams, greater expectations. Those who tied those expectations to faith in God can find the inner struggles to be enormous.

In many ways, it is not possible to understand where you are in life unless you know where you are from. With that thought in mind, let me encourage you to reflect on the era in which you grew up. That is where you formed your first notions about what life should be. Every generation has its own myths, and ours were birthed in Davy Crockett coonskin hats and set under some bright star in the heavens, the Age of Aquarius. Knowing that—and knowing what it means—can help you come to terms with disappointed dreams.

Allow yourself, then, a moment of nostalgia to look for your roots in the following generational quiz. Perhaps you'll find a measure of comfort as you discover your experiences in the present to be part of a much larger picture. Others have had and are having similar responses as they muddle their way through the middle of life. That awareness can keep you from feeling all alone—and a bit crazy.

1. Do you remember the debut of Barbie and Batman?   YES NO

2. Can you give the names of the Cartwright brothers from the television show Bonanza?   YES NO

3. Do you have a sharp mental picture of the dressed-and-pressed image of Beaver and Wally's mother, June?   YES NO

4. Can you remember a few lines from Lovin' Spoonful's "Do You Believe in Magic?" or Simon and Garfunkel's "Sounds of Silence?"   YES NO

5. Do the "good ol' days" seem more pleasant to you than the ones you're experiencing now?   YES NO

6. Do you ever feel like a victim of your times?   YES NO

7. Are you ever anxious or depressed?   YES NO

8. Do you ever feel as if you deserved something you didn't get or got something you didn't deserve?   YES NO

9. Do you remember your youth as a basically happy time with some big dreams that have gone mostly unrealized?   YES NO

10. Have you eaten a Dove Bar?   YES NO

11. Do you ever find yourself trying to make up for the big things you can't have by indulging in the little things you can?   YES NO

12. Have you changed jobs or locations often?   YES NO

13. Are you threatened by long-term, intimate relationships?   YES NO

14. Do you use vacations, shopping trips, or videos to cheer you up?   YES NO

15. Do you buy too much on credit?   YES NO

16. Do you ever wonder if you're becoming cynical and withdrawn, suspicious of advertising, government policy, and big financial appeals? YES NO

17. Do you ever feel as if, deep down, there's no one you can trust but yourself? YES NO

18. Did you embrace social and spiritual ideals at a young age—such as making your life count for something significant or changing society for the better—and now you sometimes wonder what happened to all of that? YES NO

If you answered yes to a good many of those questions, congratulate yourself. You are a product of your times. And if, like me, you hate being stereotyped and lumped into someone else's statistical glob, take courage. You are merely discovering a few of your basic tendencies and inclinations, which, though rooted in your past, have bearing on your present and your future.

As I've thought about my own life and listened to others, I've discovered that our individual stories, or lives, have been shaped much more than we realize by the times in which we've lived. Vast numbers of us began with high hopes and great expectations and have been stung as those hopes and expectations have shrunk to smaller, more lifelike size. A great collection of us thought that if we worked hard and believed well, if we followed our dreams, the road would rise to meet us. Adding faith in an all-powerful God to that formula simply baptized the whole equation. And, as we'll see, it set us up for a tremendous fall.

Real Lives, Real Stories

Though the facts that surround the journey of our generation are well-chronicled in fancy marketing strategies and predictions for our future, it is *the lives of individuals* that are most interesting. The real story is told in how we have grappled with our original dreams, relationships, and hopes for change. Growing up and growing older has thrust upon us struggles with careers and marriages, uncertainties about our faith and selves—very little of which we expected.

Our story cannot be told sufficiently in divorce statistics and income projections. We may be less political, less rich, and less trusting than most people expected, but there is much more to our story. What have we, as individuals, done with all those big dreams, with our longing to make a difference? Where are we *now* as we meander through midlife?

No one lets go of old dreams or false illusions easily. I hope to share with you the struggles and hard-won spiritual insights of people who count themselves among the postwar generation. I want to concentrate on a few in particular. Out of many possibilities I have chosen four individuals.

The first, Ted, is a man in his mid-thirties who owns a floral business. He has battled his way through near-bankruptcy in a city in much greater need of new jobs than fresh flowers. His struggle centers around the realization that he may never be able to taste success the way he'd hoped. But he has learned to taste a measure of it by just hanging in there.

A sharp-looking man with prematurely gray hair, Ted has two qualities that are particularly impressive. The first is his genuineness. In the confusing world of owning your own business, Ted has been quick to face his mistakes and admit his failures. He doesn't try to paint a glossy picture of his life. The second quality is his sheer perseverance. He has stuck it out in a difficult situation long after other people would have thrown in the towel. If anyone has deserved to do well, it is Ted.

Susan is almost ten years older. She works in public relations for a company headquartered in the Northwest, where she lives with her two daughters. What Susan wanted most out of life was an intimate, lasting relationship. Fifteen years ago she married a man she met in college, a man whose spiritual zeal took him on to seminary. There the emotional instability of his background surfaced, leaving Susan to raise two girls alone.

Susan is a woman with a great deal to give. She has only recently gained an awareness of herself and a deeper understanding of others. She no longer believes that what best cures a man's ills is a good woman.

Some of us have reached the goals, the dreams we set out to reach. Such is the case of Grant, a tall, lanky psychiatrist with a booming counseling practice and national recognition. Grant is a good example of the most curious kind of disappointment to be found in our generation. He got what he thought he wanted, only to discover that it wasn't what he wanted after all.

Grant spends his days with a steady stream of people who need someone to help them sort out the pieces of their tangled lives. He returns home—too late, he says—to a wife and four children who want a husband and father who has time for them, too. Where does Grant get the boost that everyone else looks to him for? That's a question he asks himself as he races through his days, sometimes honking at his own taillights.

And last, my own story. I grew up in a small town in Virginia with one high school—a town where no one locked his car doors and anyone would take your check. A town so vanilla in entertainment that the lives of its adults centered on sports programs, budding romances, and their children's wedding showers. The message that came through loud and clear was, "You're special, we're behind you, you go out there and knock 'em dead." My children wish we would take them back there to live. I tell them that, although I had a great support system, it made for some harsh encounters with the real world later on.

As an adult, or some facsimile thereof, I have lived with the illusion that I would someday get set in life. I could then sit back and coast because one of my many achievements would have put me over the top. It hasn't. I have been deeply committed to the idea that if you worked hard enough, or trusted God enough, then anything was possible. It isn't. Taking no for an answer is not my style. Facing disappointment and letting go of my big dreams has not been easy.

These four stories, as well as the other stories in this book, represent the individuals in our generation who, in some unseen way, attached many of their expectations of life to their concept of trusting God. As their stories unfold, you will be able to observe the process by which a person begins to bring his or her expectations in line with reality. When we come face-to-face with our disappointments, it affects our closest relationships, our whole notion of the good life, our appreciation for the role we play in a larger world. We discover that it is possible not only go grow up, but to grow beyond our dreams into a tangible sense of gratitude and a joy in the adventure of living life as we find it.

I invite you to join me in this trek in a personal but generational journey through time. You will see how disillusionment can often lead to something better—a genuine appreciation for the tentative, trusting nature of a life lived with God. Many of us have traded hype and naïveté for reality, which tastes pretty good when all is said and done.

Perhaps you have already made this transition. If so, what follows should encourage you to keep pressing on. On the other hand, you may be discouraged or depressed by seeing your aspirations dying before your eyes. In that case, I hope this book opens for you a new vista, a new way to see as you move into the future.

Regardless of your circumstances, you will likely be able to hear your own voice spoken here through someone else, and in their stories you will find a measure of your own.

When the Olympics were on . . . , I preferred to see them by myself. I cried through every single event—track, swimming, gymnastics. I just wish I could become one of them. I wish I could have been a phenomenon.

Jane Pasturlak, 33

2

Less Than We Bargained For

The Postwar Generation Grows Up

If you made a mosaic of baby boomers in their teens and twenties and compared it to one of us now, what would it look like?

One primary difference would be the change of color. The bright hues and ever-present rainbows of our youth now come in somber shades of grey and brown.

Our youth was marked by bright faces and promising futures, and the world seemed almost within our grasp. There were no immovable obstacles in our path—none that couldn't be overcome, anyway. Like newly chosen people, we lived under the blessing of God, protected against hurt, loss, and failure.

Now, twenty-five years later, we get a different picture. The jeans are tighter, the bodies inside them have gone south, and no amount of makeup can camouflage the hairline wrinkles on our faces. Mortgages and teenagers and briefcases full of paperwork have weighted down the old bounce in our step. "Underneath all my busyness," says one mother and accountant in her thirties, "I find I am mostly just very tired, and a bit bewildered with my life." Gone are the bell-bottoms and the catchy religious jargon of our youth. The world around us is still waiting to be changed. But getting the world inside our own four walls under control has proved to be its own challenge.

The '60s gave way to the individualistic '70s, the greedy '80s, and the panicky '90s. Somewhere in all the froth and foment, easy notions of marriage and family, job security and personal ambitions, and where God fit in the whole picture were severely shaken. The illusion of having it all —well-oiled careers, enough money, quality time with the children, the opportunity to travel—seems more of a myth all the time. Many of us are still playing an internal game of musical chairs, still scrambling to find the Right Job. The sheer force of our numbers has created a bottleneck in middle management and decreased the number of job openings. Career plans have plateaued or stalled in mid-flight, sometimes just when we were within range of our goal

The acronym that best fits most people our age is one coined by Ron Katz: MOSS—Middle-aged, Overstressed, Semiaffluent, Suburbanite. Katz says that the average person in our age group is forty-one years old, more overstressed than overworked, and affluent in the loosest sense of the word. We have watched our take-home earnings steadily dwindle for almost twenty years, while the average price of the most sought-after prize in the American Dream, one's own home, has risen to slightly more than $100,000.

Coupled with the economic strain is that added pressure that comes from the breakdown in the family. Our generation is generally credited with the skyrocketing divorce rate, which has ushered an array of blended families, stepfamilies, and single-parent homes into our society.

We are frequently referred to as "the sandwich generation," caught between competing demands and desires. Our children need parenting, our aging parents need attention, and our jobs require more effort for the same income. We are torn between trumped-up ideals we're no longer sure we trust and the longing for a vision. We still want our lives to make a difference, to leave behind more than a marble grave marker. Without a doubt, most of us face our middle years with a sense of how complicated and unpredictable life can turn out to be, and with ample cause for anxiety and stress.

Indeed, the years have sneaked up on us and, although they have been kinder to some than to others, they have gone by quickly. Doesn't it seem like yesterday that you were listening to "California Dreaming" while you relaxed carefree and dug your toes into the warm summer sand? Now you have to turn up the radio to hear it over the din of the kid's car pool on the "Only Oldies" station. It has been a short jaunt from the person you were to the person you are, between the dreams and hopes of then and the present reality of now.

The realization that we are no longer young seems to strike people, as it did me, at odd, unguarded moments. One woman claimed that she first felt her age when she took her daughter to a New Kids on the Block concert and realized that the only people in the audience who were sitting down were parents her age. "We would meet in the rest room," she explained, "and ask each other what on earth we were doing here. Didn't we walk out of a Rolling Stones concert just yesterday?"

Dave Barry, the humor columnist who wrote a book about the perils of turning forty, said, "I've been hanging around with people roughly my own age for the bulk of my life, and I frankly do not feel that, as a group, we have acquired the wisdom and maturity needed to run the world, or even necessarily power tools."[1] He's convinced that many of us only look like grown-ups.

A Southern homemaker and mother of three admits that when she looks in the mirror she sees someone who looks as old as she remembers her mother looking when she was a child. Sometimes the image startles her because on the inside she doesn't "feel that grown-up yet." Cheryl Merser, in her book about life passages of the postwar generation, writes that though we have indeed grown up, "we still feel somehow that real adults are in a different category;

more certain of their place in the world, wiser, their lives intact in ways we do not yet understand."[2] She says that we are grownups still in search of that inner sense of being fully adult.

Looking More Together Than We Feel

Although we've managed to live longer in adolescence than any generation preceding us, we have indeed gotten older. There are a few notable characteristics that depict our lives now, twenty-five years after that youthful era of great expectations.

For one thing, the evidence suggests that we have a highly developed ability to look more together than we feel. We know what it takes to make a good impression, how to dress for success, when to say all the right words. We have acquired many of the props of middle age— things such as insurance policies and riding lawn mowers— that make life feel easier and more secure. But underneath our polished appearance, our anxiety and confusion suggest a very different story.

We are the first generation to make happiness a goal, yet it is *our* numbers that have swelled the statistics of depression and suicide. We have virtually created the psychotherapy industry, the number of psychiatrists and psychiatric social workers having tripled since we came of age. The recent explosion in small group therapy and study groups reflects our driving need to find a listening ear, someone to offer insight into the complexities of our lives. Much more is happening inside than our efficient, congenial demeanor would suggest. We often appear to be doing better than we actually are.

A professional woman of thirty-eight who keeps a busy schedule admits that she often finds herself studying her contemporaries from a distance, wondering if they share any of her personal misgivings. She wonders if they ever allow the mildew to grow like mushrooms in their shower stalls or question whether they have the nerve to go back to school and try an entirely new field. Yet she knows that with her laptop computer and designer clothes she appears every bit as confident and self-assured as her friends and co-workers. So she turns to therapists and her husband and a small Bible study group for solace.

Sometimes that fragile world beneath the surface peeks out when we would normally expect to be at our peak performance. Grant, the psychologist, discovered that when he was asked to present his paper on sexual abuse at a national consortium of mental health professionals. It was an opportunity that represented a reward for his success, a chance-of-a-lifetime event. Yet he found himself ambivalent about the prospect of presenting his findings. He began waking up in the middle of the night wondering if he could really pull it off. Did he have all the data he needed? Were his case studies sufficiently documented? He knew that for the most part they were unreasonable fears, and he was dismayed to be plagued by the same anxiety he observed in some of his patients.

Such anxiety is peculiar to individuals whose successful appearance causes them to fear that some big event will reveal them to be the very opposite. They are afraid of being discovered as inadequate and lacking. The label given to this fear is "The Imposter Phenomenon,"[3] a term coined from research among high achievers, especially in our generation. It refers to the self-doubt that dogs the steps of people like Grant, who for all appearances should be free of such insecurities.

Grant's life is an example of the kind of stress and constant demand that many of us carry—stress that takes its toll beneath well-fashioned appearances. Grant supervises a clinic, attends meetings of professional groups, spends time with his wife and four children, and participates in church activities. His wife tells him that he's pushing too hard, but he doesn't know how to relax. "I need time to process all that is happening around me," he says, "to sort through my own affairs. But I rarely find such time, unless you count midnight to two A.M." Yet only those closest to him could guess how stretched he feels. He has years of professional bedside manner to disguise his own uneasiness.

In her book *Passages,* Gail Sheehy explains why mid-life is often marked by an inner restlessness and uncertainty.[4] Part of the reason we look more together than we feel is that the middle years of life require us to do so much personal reevaluation. It is the time of reassessment. Have we done what we hoped to do? What exactly were our original hopes and dreams, and how does our life stack up against them?

Sheehy quotes famous people from other eras to remind us how universal that interior struggle is. Eleanor Roosevelt on her thirty-fifth birthday complained that she never felt less confident in her life. The philosopher Dante wrote that "in the middle of his journey he came to a dark wood where the straight way was lost."

Every generation must accept dashed dreams and the confusion that often marks the process of growing older. But for those born after World War II, in an era of such inflated hopes, the task is even harder. Because our expectations were so high to begin with, we have had much farther to fall.

In my twenties I felt nearly invincible, a kind of religious I-am-woman-hear-me-roar. The usual initiatory rites of adulthood had been easy enough to attain. I finished school, got married, put my husband through seminary while I taught, and near the end of the school year rushed to the hospital to deliver our first child. I thought hard work and determination could take me almost anywhere.

Not until I was in my thirties did I recognize, in a personal sense, that I was struggling with inner feelings and doubts that did not always match the confident image I projected.

My wide-eyed enthusiasm, my own set of great expectations, began to disintegrate in the cold astringent of real life. The ministry for which my husband and I had spent years in preparation carried as many headaches and disap-

pointments as joys. Both of our children were getting older, and it was more evident each day that neither would
grow up to be president. I began to see the frailty and humanness in some of my spiritual heroes, Christians I had
looked up to in the past. The goals I had worked so hard to
achieve only left me with more to reach for. I felt let down,
as though the old sense of wonder and anticipation had
completely evaporated from my life. I wanted to say, "You
mean, this is the way life turns out? This is it? What have I
missed? Surely there's more!"

Alone in a Crowd

Another characteristic of the postwar generation is
that we are intensely aware of a longing for relationship;
for a sense of connection with God, with other people,
even with ourselves. Perhaps one explanation is that having been herded together from our youth, the need and
desire for strong relationships has been built in to us.

Whatever the reason, we have not achieved much of
that desired goal. We are strangely lonely people. As the
song says in the sitcom "Cheers," it would be nice to go
someplace where everybody knows your name—if we could
just find out where that is. Here especially, in this relational
arena, reality has fallen far short of our expectations.

Jack Skeen, a Baltimore psychologist whose practice
is inundated with patients between the ages of twenty-five
and forty-five, explains: "Almost to a person, there is a
loneliness in this age group, a hungering to be understood. In spite of their accomplishments and their past relationships, they have rarely found anyone who understands that loneliness or acknowledges the part of them
that's unique and personal. I think that in many ways they
are a very powerless generation, easily swayed by advertising, yet because of their numbers, often overlooked as individuals."

The longing for intimacy may have been a hidden motivation behind much of what we have accomplished. Our

culture seems to hold forth the implicit promise that if you apply yourself—if you overcome the obstacles—the carrot at the end of the stick is shaped in the form of a person. If you chew Wrigleys' gum you will double your pleasure and double your fun—and double your chances to meet an attractive woman. The goal behind the goal is a lasting, intimate relationship, a personal sense of family.

Therein lies the rub. You can win the Nobel Prize and celebrate that fact essentially alone. There is little direct connection between accomplishment and relationship. "Many in this age group have indeed applied themselves," Skeen says, "only to realize through depression or marital problems or unrelenting singleness that all their hard work hasn't fulfilled the aching, lonely void of unmet relational needs. They long for someone to care about them as a person—to matter just for who they are."

"I haven't really had close friends since I was in high school," confides one editor in her early forties. "It's not that I wouldn't love to have some now, but I don't know who it's safe to talk to at work. You never know how people will read you or what they might repeat."

Another computer whiz, who is also a single father, says, "Sometimes I feel like I live in a state of emotional vertigo. Most of the time I'm just spinning around in circles, carrying out a list of tasks, connected to no one."

An emotional, relational shriveling takes place when our lives move so fast, and the stress is so heavy and thick that we cannot forge the friendships and connections we need. Many of us are long on associations and short on relationships. One pastor admits, "When the Million Dollar Roundtable of young business executives asked me to speak, I was amazed at the topic they requested. Friendships. These people can do all sorts of things, but they don't know how to build lasting friendships."

An Episcopal priest agrees: "Most people in this generation live in their own isolated boxes in the suburbs, a thousand miles away from family, in communities in which they feel no roots. They are plagued by loneliness, yet driven by demanding jobs and competing family needs. Underneath all that activity is a deep longing for connection with God that seems real and intimate."

A person can be lonely even within the closest of relationships, but those who experience the demand and isolation of single parenting feel it quite acutely. By the turn of the century, more than half of our generation will have experienced divorce at least once, many more than once. Two-thirds of the children we gave birth to in the '80s will spend some time with a single parent.[5] The toll of single parenting—of singleness in general—creates its own relational vacuum.

Susan's story is a classic case in point. When she was thinking of marrying Jim, that relationship symbolized certainty to her. She met him in college, in the context of a campus ministry, and she hoped, as we all do, to find in him a soul mate, a friend, as well as a husband.

They hadn't been married long, however, before problems started to surface. "Within the first two years," Susan says, "I realized that Jim was battling a lot of old ghosts in his personal life. His relationship with his dad was a continual source of pressure for him. His compulsion to prove himself made him a driven man." Hidden reefs seemed to block any real hope of being close.

Soon Jim was elected president of his seminary class. He also became the youngest elder in their church. In many ways, Jim was simply too talented for his own good. No one realized that the image he projected was incongruent with the man inside or that his lifelong inability to gain his father's affirmation was an inner sore that still festered.

Jim's ministry flourished, his performance serving to deflect attention from his inner needs. He confided to his pastor that he was struggling with an attraction to pornography, but his pastor didn't take him seriously. And the church was growing so rapidly that Jim and Susan got lost in the crowd.

Eventually Jim decided to drop out of seminary and go back to the business world. But Susan suspected hidden motives behind his decision. Jim began to travel more and more in his job. Susan wondered if something was wrong, and when he began staying out half the night, becoming as emotionally distant as he was physically absent, her concern grew.

The advice she received from other Christians was confusing. If Susan could just be a better, sexier, more encouraging wife, they said, her husband would return to his normal self. The trouble was, he didn't.

When Jim left—or more accurately, when Susan finally insisted that Jim get help and he left—more than a marriage and a family was shattered. It would take a number of years to rebuild Susan's ability to trust people, to trust her own judgment, and to learn what it meant to trust God.

For more than ten years, Susan has been rasing her two girls alone. "I've gotten over the tendency to be apologetic when I say I'm divorced," she says. "I am divorced, and that's the reality of it all. And part of that reality is a kind of loneliness that creeps in—in little ways and big ways—in the way I sense my girls need a father. There is no one to share the load of responsibility for parenting two children, no one who can pick up for me when I get tired. Between my job and my children's activities there is little time left to pursue the kind of friendships that would provide more of the support I need at this point in my life. Loneliness is a persistent struggle for me—one that I live with in a daily way."

So with the challenges of singleness, of lives that move too fast, of relationships that produce acquaintances when we long for friendships, there are many in our generation who are painfully aware of feeling alone—even in a crowd.

Down the Up Escalator

Another way in which our lives are different than we expected is our economic status. The good times of the '50s and the '60s became, for many, the tight times of the '70s, '80s, and '90s. "I feel that there's a life I was raised to have," one man said, "and financially I just haven't been able to make that happen." The subtitle of Christopher Lasch's 1979 best-seller *The Culture of Narcissism* reads *American Life in an Age of Diminishing Expectations.*

We have moved from the implicit promise of an upward mobility to the stark possibility of going down the up escalator. The image of the yuppie in a business suit sprinting up the courthouse steps, briefcase in hand, is largely a creation of the media. Although his numbers will increase slightly in the '90s, many of us can barely pay our bills. The majority will earn less, in real income, at every age than did the generation that preceded us. For "younger boomers" (ages twenty-eight through thirty-seven), economic realities have been particularly harsh. Their house payments can be twice the size of the older group, their discretionary funds considerably less, and many of the best jobs gone before they arrive on the scene.

The guarantees in the system, real or implied, no longer exist. Instead, the cracks are widening, and no amount of electric coffee grinders or compact disc players can prevent our slipping through them. We have mortgages to pay and too much credit card debt. In a few short years, the hot career field of today may be overcrowded and obsolete. In fact, most people in this age group will shift into new careers, not once or twice, but more than three times in a lifetime.

No matter how hard we try, most of us have not been able to recreate the safe, tidy lives that we remember our parents having. Though we are the largest group of college-educated Americans to date, that statistic may have served only to line the entrance lobby with far too many applicants for each job.

It seemed easy—too easy—maybe—for our parents' generation, as though they collectively possessed the Midas Touch. In the twenty-five years that followed World War II, our parents saw their real purchasing power double, a phenomenon not seen before or since. I remember one likable man in my hometown, the local football coach, who made a smooth transition from football to selling millions of dollars of life insurance to returning WWII veterans. Another, a local banker, built a modest apartment building at low interest rates. When he retired, he sold those twelve units for more than he made in a lifetime in his full-time profession. You have to work hard to find stories like that in our generation.

Ted, the same guy who recruited half his fraternity to hear a Christian speaker in college, was not prepared for the uphill struggle he encountered in the floral business. Friends had always told him that he had a natural gift for making money. By the age of twenty-five, when his peers were barely thinking beyond the upcoming weekend, Ted was busy buying small houses during the real estate boom of the '70s.

He had never been a stranger to hard work. Though he could have rested on his parent's affluence, he was the son who found his own job in a paint store at the age of fourteen. He had grown up expecting to work hard, and he had expected that hard work would pay off.

The fact that Ted had become a Christian in college only deepened his desire to go into business. He used to daydream about being part of a group of businessmen committed to incarnating their witness in what was often a competitive, compromising environment.

The floral business was a natural match for Ted's abilities. He started out packing boxes with flowers at the largest wholesale florist in Chicago; within a few years he managed an entire division. Like a walking inventory sheet, he had a rare ability to store mammoth amounts of numbers in his head. Yet he was a salesman as well, as comfortable working with people as with invoices.

Ted sailed through his first year of owning his own business. Inside, he couldn't help congratulating himself just a little. He was on the verge of grabbing hold of a long-awaited dream.

Then, in the time it takes to feel the wind shift, everything changed. A cloud of unemployment and business slowdown began to envelop what had previously been a prosperous region. Suddenly consumers decided they could do without flowers. The floral shops that were Ted's clients began placing smaller and smaller orders.

"When I first went to the bank to see about a loan for this business," Ted says, "there was another man waiting as well, and he had been in business for two years. Right away he started telling me about employees who wanted to sue him, about his problems with computers and the IRS and tax people and lawyers, about his struggles with cash flow, collections, and sleep. I thought to myself, *Boy, I can't relate to this at all.*"

Ted looks back on that conversation now as having been somewhat prophetic, as he soon discovered what it was like to have everything he touched turn to ashes—not gold. He is only one of the many whose career and financial goals were downsized by a shrinking economy and abrupt reversals of fortune; whose secret fear is that they may go down what was supposed to be an up escalator.

Gaining Perspective

"You've come a long way, baby," sang the Virginia Slims commercials. Indeed, we have. In a little more than two decades we have seen many of our great expectations evaporate before our eyes. We have both inherited and created a world much more complex and uncertain than we ever imagined. As columnist P. J. O'Rourke wrote, "'We are the world,' we shouted just a couple of years ago. And just a couple of years ago we were. How did we wind up so old? So fat? So confused? So broke?"[6]

Twenty-five years ago, the spiritually idealistic among us linked our dreams—in a veiled way—to our understanding of God and what it meant to follow Him. We were introduced to an all-powerful God; not some nebulous entity devoid of definition, but a God who had invaded history in the person of Jesus Christ, a God who could be known. The times in which we were living and the way we heard the message meant that, in many cases, we only believed all the more deeply that our goals and dreams were attainable. The fact that our lives were linked to the God of the universe was like wind beneath our feet allowing us to soar in life where others stalled. We would leap where others only stumbled along. "God loved us and had a wonderful plan for our lives," and our belief in Him seemed to put us in a special category of immunity and protection. In our youthful minds, there was no understanding of or preparation for hardships that refused to go away and pain that required time to heal. As a result, we have felt our disappointments more deeply than our unbelieving brothers and sisters.

Like Susan and Ted—even Grant in less obvious ways—divorce and business failures, insecurity and dissatisfaction, were not part of our mental concept of the abundant life in Christ. Consequently, we have found the task of sorting out old dreams and coming to terms with life, as we near and pass the age of "frantic forty," to be a much greater challenge than we anticipated.

That sorting-out process, so common to anyone between the ages of thirty-five and forty-five, requires that we look back into our past as well as forward into our future. It is like coming to the crest of a hill and looking in both directions while standing at the top. For those whose dreams were even loosely attached to their faith, the need to look backward is imperative.

Indeed, where we are now as individuals—and in a larger sense, as a generation—is rooted in where we have been. Our childhoods and the era of the '60s played a huge role in establishing the disappointments that have come since. There, amidst hula hoops and super-heroes, we gave birth to our great expectations.

We consciously think of ourselves as different from those people who came before.

Walt Harrison, 41

3

The Children of Promise

Tracing the Birth of Our Great Expectations

On a cloudless afternoon two summers ago, I boarded a plane bound for Minneapolis. In no time the plane climbed to cruising altitude, and I sat back in my seat and relaxed. It was a perfect day for flying.

By the time we neared Minneapolis I was lost in conversation with a nine-year-old Malaysian boy, fluent in English, who told me everything I had ever wanted to know about his country—and then some. I failed to notice how long we had been circling the airport, or the strained silence of the passengers. Just as I started to feel vaguely nauseous—you can only go around in circles so long—we began our descent.

The plane touched ground, and curiously enough, spontaneous applause rippled through the passengers. *What a warm, responsive group,* I thought. White trucks with strobe red lights lined the runway beside our plane. How remarkable. The conscientious airport had fire drills even on Sundays.

Not until I got to baggage claim and chanced to overhear another passenger say he was just glad to be alive did I start to suspect anything. I ventured a naive question: "Pardon me, but I was on that plane. Was there something wrong?"

He peered at me over his beard as if I had been locked in the rest room with my headphones on. "Lady," he said, in carefully measured words. "Lady, didn't you hear that pilot? The plane's wheels wouldn't come down for a full half hour. We almost landed in that field out there." I sheepishly gathered my bags and headed down the concourse, thankful that I *hadn't* heard what the pilot said. In the back of my mind, echoes from the past, voices of the little rascals in my childhood neighborhood, reminded me that I was something of a space cadet after all.

I am still amazed that I could have spent the last hour of that trip so thoroughly unaware of the predicament I was in. Surely there had been enough airplane disasters to make one wary. Yet somehow my unbridled optimism remained intact. I successfully overlooked even the most obvious warning signs because I had never expected to encounter anything but an uneventful ride, a smooth sail to where I wanted to go.

In the past few years, as I've observed the disillusionment many people face in midlife, that plane ride often comes to mind. When we started out, the prospects for the future were sunny, hopeful, reassuring. We were flying the friendly skies of Eisenhower or Kennedy's America. Wars and recessions were part of the past; few prophets foresaw a shrinking economy or the pressures that would confront families of the '90s.

Twenty-year-olds always have stars in their eyes, big dreams, and great hopes for the future. But for our generation, the good times of the '50s and '60s made for an even greater sense of expectation, an illusion of guarantees. This was the buildup that led to such a letdown and to frustration that simmers just beneath the surface.

We have encountered far more turbulence than we planned for on this trip: dissolving marriages, double-digit inflation, job scarcity, internal stress, and persistent loneliness that our parents' generation could have hardly imagined. It's shaky out there—and sometimes it's a bit shaky "in here" too.

Childhood Cocoons

When you set out to discover where and how you first formed notions about what you could expect on this flight through life, you inevitably end up sorting through the relics of your childhood. There, surrounded by Mickey Mouse hats and Beatles records, we formed many of our impressions about what we could expect out of life.

Social researchers point out that somewhere around your tenth year, your values and outlook, your expectations, are forged into definable shape. Between the ages of ten and twenty you just test and confirm your original values. After that, it will require considerable pain or payoff to alter those values.

Young eyes and minds absorb far more than they appear to. It's as though you take a hard look at what's happening around you, digest the messages coming from TV, your parents, the kid next door, and you say, "This is the way life *is*. This is the way life will be."

Do you remember where you were and what you were doing at the tender age of ten? Can you focus on that slice of life and interpret what you surmised about the world from your relationships and circumstances at that time?

When I play back the tape of memories in my mind, I stop on a warm spot around my tenth year and find myself sitting beside the red clay bank that surrounded our home, a gallon pickle jar of water beside me. I would sit on the side of the mountain for hours, with the sun warming my back as I molded pots out of the Indian dirt. I loved the squishy, malleable quality of the clay, the way it took shape beneath the pressure of my fingers. That image accurately summarizes my childhood assumptions about life. I believed that with enough skill and effort, I could shape the forces and events of my life as readily as that red clay.

But I wasn't alone on that hill. About ten of us ran together as a herd all over the side of that mountain, building hideouts deep in the woods, oblivious to the thought of danger. "Crime" was limited, in our minds, to the streets of Harlem, a mythical evil necessary to thicken the plot of "Dragnet."

Occasionally we checked in with our mothers, none of whom were June Cleavers, but they were present, maybe too involved with their children's lives. And divorce? There were no single-parent homes on our hill. Our parents might have argued a bit, but *divorce*—that word was unknown to our vocabularies until much later. Whatever might have actually been missing from our family relationships (and judging from the current number of Adult Children of Alcoholics and sexual abuse support groups, it was quite a lot), on the surface at least, the image of togetherness was intact.

Susan looks back on her childhood as a part of her life that was almost too good to be true. Her dad made a comfortable living managing a local chain of bookstores in a community where family roots were measured not in years but in generations, where no one locked his doors unless he left for a two-week vacation. She admits that her family relationships were shallow, with most difficulties well hidden beneath a pleasant veneer that served to protect her from the messier, more painful side of life.

She is grateful for the good times of her childhood. But she is quick to add that her sheltered background made the hard knocks of divorce doubly difficult. "I realize now how unprepared I was for life," Susan says. "My marriage falling apart was the first major incidence in my life of realizing that not everyone you trust deserves such trust. After Jim left, I felt like I'd been catapulted out of a cocoon."

So our bright childhoods were probably more image than substance, but that aura of security and privilege shaped our unrealistic expectations for the future. Even now, when we flip the radio dial to the nostalgic music of that era, it's the magic, as much as the music, that draws us.

Different Childhoods, Different Values

We need only to compare our parents' orientation (the War Generation) to our own (the Boom Generation) to realize that a person's early perceptions of life filter his whole outlook. Never has so much diversity existed simultaneously in the same century, affording us the chance to observe how important those early experiences really are.[1]

The fine irony is that our experience is practically the reverse of our parents'. The hardest years of their lives were, for the most part, their early years—the proving ground from which they moved on to better things. They may have grown up in the Great Depression and fought in World War II, but when they returned they were able to build lives that were beyond their wildest hopes.

Yet we have to ask, Didn't our parents encounter disappointments, too, as they moved from adolescence to adulthood? Didn't they have dreams and illusions they were forced to let go of? Undoubtedly they did. Every generation has its youthful idealism. But in their case, the two major events of their childhood and adolescence came to their aid. The Depression and World War II taught them that hardship and sacrifice were part of many unpleasant possibilities that might come their way. They knew that life was not easy.

Because of their earlier experiences, they were more informed of reality. The Great Depression was more than a story handed down from the generation before—they had lived through it. They watched or were among the able-bodied young men leaving for the shores of the Pacific or the battlefields of Europe, many of whom would never return.

So although the War Generation left adolescence harboring its own set of dreams, those dreams were tempered by previous experience, and as a result, they were able to deal with life as it came to them. Many more of their dreams did materialize, and even when some didn't, the discrepancy between them and reality was not as great as ours.

Our parents' early memories are filled with the haggard faces of men in search of work. They lived with scarcity and need and the insecurity of not knowing whether the family would have to sell the farm or move to a new community to find work. As a result of growing up in a time when one could hardly plan for the future because the present was so tenuous, the War Generation has always placed a high premium on *stability.* They are more cautious and conservative, unwilling to count any chickens before they hatch. There is a right way to worship and raise children. Everything has a place and needs to be there. Predictability and security are paramount.

Whereas our generation has accentuated the distinctiveness of the individual, our parents have placed value on the power of the group. It took a team effort to pull out of the Depression and to win a war. The individual sublimated his own desires in favor of a larger good; he put his shoulder to the wheel and didn't ask questions. And any good team has a strong leader as implicitly trustworthy as Dwight Eisenhower or Douglas MacArthur. For our parents, commitment to authority and institutions has been a given since their childhood.

They have been criticized for not taking time to smell the roses, but nothing in their formative years allowed for such leisure. Hard work has prevailed as the queen of virtues for them, and it's no wonder, since it was work, work, and more work that eventually ushered in an era of unprecedented prosperity.

Great Beginnings

Unfortunately, we would have to take our parents' childhoods and life experiences and turn them upside down if we wanted them to match our own. The best years of our lives have been, for the most part, the first years of our lives.[2] There was little reason to think that the future held anything but more of the same. It is for good reason that the Hebrew wisdom of the Old Testament states, "It is good for a man to bear the yoke while he is young."[3] We are better off if life goes from worse to better, rather than from better to worse.

When Ted speaks of his background he explains that he grew up hearing his parents' stories about how hard life was in the Depression and how hard they had worked all their lives. "That's exactly where I got my impression that all my hard work would pay off as handsomely for me as theirs did for them," he says. Ted was raised in a Dutch family in New England where father had passed onto son the virtues of thrift and labor through many generations.

Just as surely as the cart follows the horse, Ted expected each generation of his family to grow more prosperous. He had nothing to prepare him for the hard work that paid off simply by keeping the creditors from the door.

When we think of the factors in our childhoods that fueled our great expectations, one holds particular influence: our numbers. There were so many of us. Seventy-six million babies, toddlers, school children, and teenagers—a huge spotlight was focused on this bulging herd of humanity. We had new elementary schools, new textbooks, new station wagons, all bought or built to accommodate record numbers of children born in the wake of America's victory euphoria.

Our size made us an irresistibly large market, tracked by invisible men with clipboards (market researchers they were called), who followed us around, noting our preferences. On their advice, forests were denuded in search of raccoon tails for Davy Crockett hats. Their commercial savvy gave us plastic rings called "hula hoops," producing as many as 20 million a day until one month in 1959 the market turned and no one could give a hula hoop away.

Imperceptibly the preferences of our generation began to dominate culture. Instead of adopting our parents' choices and opinions, we established our own. Mass-produced hamburgers, Weejuns, and miniskirts were tailored to our tastes. We made rock music everyone's music. We danced to it, got married to it, and those of use who can afford to will retire on Florida beaches and tap our arthritic toes to it. Whatever the item, if we liked it, someone got rich; when we cast it aside, someone went broke.

That is a lot of power to rest in the hands of one group of people. When McDonald's told us that we needed a break today and Burger King said we could have it our way, we knew they were singing our song. We ate instant oatmeal and watched Polaroid pictures develop before our eyes. Television, that ubiquitous metal and glass box in the corner of the living room, deceptively portrayed a life-style that was, in fact, three times the average American income. In sixty minutes any personal or global problem could be solved, and if you were bored, you simply changed the channel. We were children with endless options, and our choices came in thirty-one flavors.

One stray piece of generational trivia helps explain why we grew up with such unrealistic expectations. An unusual proportion of us were firstborns, eldest children who for a brief sparkling moment got to claim the center of their parent's attention. But as one commentator noted, the prevailing emphasis on children made a whole generation "eldest children," growing up with the idea that the "world is organized just for them."[4] We were entitled to the good life. What other generations had thought of as privileges—sending your children to college or having a secure retirement—we view as rights.

In addition to that sense of entitlement, research on birth order suggests that the firstborn is also likely to trust authority more deeply, to believe that life is orderly and the world is just. Firstborns are usually quite conscientious and expect to be rewarded for their efforts.

"I felt that I was entitled to a whole lot in life," says one Midwestern mother of two. "I was the only girl amidst three brothers and I felt very special. We lived in a nice parsonage; my family was center-stage at church.

"I remember reading in *Weekly Readers* about how we would all have helicopters. And because somebody had just invented space food, we wouldn't even have to eat. If we wanted to be president of the United States, then we could. When I was in high school, I didn't pay any attention to cheerleading and home ec—I took drafting and electronics. There was never any doubt in my mind that I could do anything I wanted to. All doors were open to me."

Gone were the days when the children existed to contribute to the family struggle for survival. Unlike our parents, who were thankful to get oranges and apples in their Christmas stockings, Santa Claus could bring us almost anything in the Sears Roebuck Catalog. Most parents strove to spare their children the austerity of their own childhoods—though not without a little instructive recall, now and then.

My mother used to describe the four miles she walked to school through the treacherous Virginia mountains. That long-ago-and-far-away glaze would cover her eyes, and I knew what was coming.

"Don't you realize," she would say, forgetting how well I realized, "that I used to walk four miles one way every day, in cold, wind, snow, sleet, and hail, to get to school?"

My brother and me she drove.

The Values of the Postwar Generation

Growing up in such a different era we developed values that differed from our parents'. Visibility, recognition, impact, and accomplishment are the things we value.

Grant, the psychiatrist, knows what that drive to stand out in a crowd is like. "On the one hand," he says, "I watched the example of my father and took note. He held a steady government job all his life, one where the promotions and raises followed like clockwork. Part of me just thought I'd grow up and take my place on the dog sled— no meteoric, rising star. Yet I have to admit that underneath those lame ambitions, there is the churning to do something remarkable. I'd like to cut a path that has been overlooked. I want to leave my own mark."

Grant claims that the longing to soar rather than just coast along is partly what propelled him into medical school and made him one of the youngest psychiatrists in his class to establish his own clinic. Yet he finds that for each goal he reaches, a new one crops up in front of him. On the other hand, the older he gets the more he sees the need to slow down, enjoy where he is, and declare enough is enough.

As individuals, we are less compelled to melt into the standard conventions prescribed by the larger group. More often we follow an internal drummer, in tune with our own instincts. The question, Why? is second nature to us. Our parents rose to the occasion when a patriotic man with a pointed finger said, "Uncle Sam wants you!" Our generation replied, "Heck, no, I won't go."

We have embarked on a long and roundabout search to *find meaning in life.* Beneath all the drivenness to accumulate more and more, we still long to grab hold of what matters—what really matters. The search for fulfillment continues, and the options multiply.

Because of that searching nature, we welcome change and variation, not as something to be feared, but as something to take advantage of. We have a low threshold for boredom. Whether it's a winter ski vacation or serving lunch in a downtown soup kitchen, we are prone to collect experiences like our parents collected coins. We embrace the new and different, always on the lookout for what adds meaning and purpose to life.

The Impact of the Sixties

Most commentators claim that our childhoods were special, and that we were left with the feeling of being special as well. You may remember the moment in *The Big Chill* when actor William Hurt, the resident philosopher, turns to his middle-aged friends and says, "Wise up, guys, no one ever had a cushier birth." It is just this "cushy birth," with its inherent sense of privilege, that fueled much of the idealism of the sixties.

From our charmed childhoods, we moved into a decade as schizophrenic as any this century has known. Two stories were simultaneously played out before our eyes, like competing television screens. One picture showed millions of students packing their bags for college, feeding off America's affluence and world position.

But the other screen was bleeding like an open wound, throbbing with the pain of Vietnam, of civil rights demonstrations, and the death of heroes. The scenes that invaded our sanitized living rooms—angry protesters and naked Vietnamese children—challenged the surface tranquility of our lives. We were caught between the threshold of fulfilling big dreams and the nagging awareness that some sinister force was astir.

Because a person's perspective on that era varies with the picture they were most tuned in to, there will always be room for differing opinions. In fact, when *Newsweek* correspondent Tom Matthews prophesied the future, he half-humorously envisions that fifty years from now, when there are only a couple dozen centenarians left, "the last liberal and the last conservative, the last lieutenant and the last draft-card burner, the last head and the last narc will undoubtedly be out on the porch at the Home trying to gum each other to death over the Last Principle."[5]

Much could be said about the sixties, yet one theme remains constant. Beneath the clamor and the dissonance, a note of idealism holds steady. In spite of Vietnam and the assassinations of three national figures, our belief that we could win the day remained intact. Not until the exposure of Watergate in 1972 did we start to settle back in our armchairs with a sigh of apathy, eventually fading into disillusionment.

Until then, it seemed that we could always get around the law of gravity—if we were clever enough. Note *Time* magazine's 1967 assessment of our potential: "In its lifetime, this promising generation could land on the moon, cure cancer and the common cold, lay out blight-proof, smog-free cities, help end racial prejudice, enrich the underdeveloped world, and, no doubt, write an end to poverty and war."[6] About the only thing left out of that list is the ability to walk on water.

To live in that era was to absorb, as if by osmosis, an optimism that fed our already oversized hopes and expectations for what life could deliver. With enough protest, or by sheer force of will, we believed that age-old social ills could be remedied. The problems that other generations had tried to chip away piece by piece, we strove to undo overnight. It was the Age of Aquarius—the dawning of a new day.

Such idealism was easy to transport. We carried it into our understanding of Christianity with some wonderful, and some not so wonderful, results. In certain ways, the heady sense of being on the front end of a tidal wave aided the Christian cause. It served to emphasize the radical nature of the gospel. *Now* was the time to make a decision for Christ, and that decision was life-changing. A person's commitment mattered; his life could make a difference in a world that needed that difference.

The intensity with which we embraced those ideas left little doubt as to the crucial importance of the claims of Christ. "When I told my parents I had become a Christian," one pastor recalls, "they said that they had just lost a son. And that hurt. But it also made me dig for an answer. I realized that if the gospel was true then it affected every area of my life—my schoolwork, my ambitions for the future, my relationship with my parents. I saw that I was staring in the face of the most significant life questions a person has to deal with."

Likewise, the great hopes we held in common produced a bonding web of relationship not to be equaled or surpassed. Many of us still count our friendships from that era among the closest we've ever experienced.

Inflated Dreams

But there was a dark side to that idealism. It carried in its wake a number of false hopes and pipe dreams. Inevitably, the big buildup had its own letdown. The most obvious of these took place en masse. We didn't change the world—all that much. Our global dreams were forced to shrink.

A half million people gathered in a farmer's field in Woodstock, their lighted candles swaying in the dark as they tried to hurry along this new era with all the emotional fervor of a religious revival. But the new day that dawned was pretty much the same as those that went before. Folk singer Alro Guthrie prophesied that all political systems were on the way out, that we were finally going to get to the point where there would be no more bigotry or war. But racism and enmity proved as hard to stamp out as brush fires in a dry forest.

Not long after Woodstock, 100,000 Christians gathered in the Cotton Bowl in Dallas, Texas, for a week called Explo '72, an event heralded as the most significant Christian happening since Pentecost. By day they sat under the broiling Texas sun, and at night they sang along with the best Christian music groups and listened to spirited messages. Afterward they stuck to the seats of crowded buses that carried them to remote suburbs to sleep on air mattresses in empty apartments—and they thought little of it.

They were part of a "conspiracy" to change the world, an army of Christians who could, by 1980, fulfill Christ's Great Commission to take the gospel to every single person on earth. We were going to change the world in our generation. *In our generation.* Remember?

A noble task in a needy world—the stuff dreams are made of. "When I look back on that era as a Christian," one educator says, "I realize what a simplistic view of the spheres of power we had. We thought we could make whatever changes needed to be made. There were no real problems that wouldn't go away." If we were clever enough, we would subdue gravity.

The idealism that had been focused on global change spilled over into our personal lives, as in Susan's case. Her hopes took the shape of a relationship—a stable, intimate marriage. That was the desire of her heart and one that seemed to align with what God would want as well. "Part of the protective bubble I lived in then," she says, "was the idea that if my dreams were good, real pain and heartache wouldn't touch me. Not deeply, anyway. The emphasis was on trusting God to work everything out, so I didn't ask too many questions beyond that. Every circumstance in my life just seemed to point to marrying Jim."

The same idealism caused us to skip lightly over the harder words of Scripture that spoke of surrender and adversity, of failure and weakness. Our backgrounds left us unprepared for the irreversible losses, the painful letting go that comes with growing up and growing older in a fallen world.

Our communal dreams were accompanied by personal assumptions, youthful illusions smuggled in until the gospel became, in part, a golden thread that would tie up the loose ends of our lives in a tidy package. We connected our personal dreams and our mental images of the good life with mustard-seed faith in a God who could move mountains. Many of our high hopes were overlaid with Bible promises, and therein lay a double sting. The apostle Paul said that God was able to do exceedingly abundantly beyond all we could ask or think. What such mammoth assurances meant to a generation of Christians with oversized aspirations, only God knows.

If He was going to do exceedingly abundantly for us, then He was in for a challenge.

PART 2

LETTING GO
OF
OLD DREAMS

The idea I absorbed was that if you did what God said, everything would come out all right in the end. What I found, though, is that the end may be a lot further down the road than you think.

Paul Borthwick, 37

4
Broken Rainbows

Acknowledging the Promises God Never Made

For the first few years after I turned thirty I was aware of a vague feeling of disappointment—a general malaise, with few symptoms and no name. It just turned up unpredictably, like recurrent mono. Or to change the metaphor, it simmered on the back burner in my mind, and as long as I kept the heat turned down, I was OK.

It was not as though something catastrophic had taken place. At the time, my husband and I were leading a collegiate ministry at a university in Oklahoma. We were hoping to see the students gain a heart for ministering overseas, but we were realizing slowly that, if you're a kid who has grown up in Oklahoma, Little Rock is a foreign country.

But there was plenty to keep a person encouraged, and for the most part, I was too busy chasing toddlers and squirreling away a few hours behind a typewriter to devote much energy to introspection. I only knew that there was a widening gap between what I had hoped for and what was actually happening in my life, and that the disillusionment had something to do with God.

That part I hated to admit. It took me a long time to see that my disappointment was tangled up with my ideas about the Christian life. Besides, the fact that I was married to a man in the ministry was a complicating factor. In that role I often felt cast as a spiritual presswoman doing public relations work for God. And that is one odd spot to be in when you are having second thoughts yourself. I couldn't understand why the "abundant life" that seemed to promise so much more—more intimacy, more impact, more satisfaction—had, in many instances, mysteriously turned out to be less.

I decided to treat my life as a video and play a few scenes backward, until I could find those private places where I had first formed mental images of how I had expected things to turn out. Only then did I discover how much my faith had been influenced by my great expectations.

The Abundant Life?

The spiritual journey of our generation had its own preconceived ideas and assumptions. When someone spoke of the abundant life in Christ, for example, what images formed in the back of our minds? *In a large sense, those expectations revolved primarily around ideas of protection and guarantee.*

Somewhere in the idea of the "abundant life" in Jesus was a strong hint of a solution to most every problem, unhampered opportunities, untroubled relationships—a life that was largely wrinkle-free *if* only you found the right Bible study or appropriate spiritual principle. Missing were the hard words such as *perseverance* and *loneliness* and *defeat.* Christianity was not so much a calling to a holy life as an invitation to a better one—an abundant life.

One woman reflects on how she mixed her dreams with notions about God: "I was so thoroughly schooled in the idea that God loved me and had a wonderful plan for my life that I was shocked, really shocked, when the first major unwonderful event took place." Another man adds, "I took a lot of false comfort in what I call the one-right-way illusion. If faced with a difficult decision, I had only to take my Bible and, like a spiritual Thoreau, retire to Walden Pond. There I would lay out the options and God would show me the supremely right one, a sort of yellow brick road that, once followed, would guarantee me of never being wrong." Somehow, it seemed that if we just Christianized our ideals we could insure them.

Those ideas did not materialize out of thin air, of course. Back in the fifties, Norman Vincent Peale contended in his best-selling book *The Power of Positive Thinking* that the Bible contained "techniques" and "formulas" that formed an exact science on how to handle your problems. There were "ten simple, workable rules" for living and "magic words" that could overcome almost anything.

By the time we reached our twenties and were trying to find our way though a new world of work and weddings and wet diapers, the pragmatic American mind-set had thoroughly taken hold. Now there was a how-to seminar or Christian self-help book on nearly every topic imaginable. If you wanted to follow a charted course of progress in Christian discipleship, there were workbooks that packaged those answers in "ten basic steps."[1] Did you need to find out how to choose a mate or manage your finances or develope a biblical worldview? There was a method or program to help you. And if you followed the rules, you could count on success.

It's not as though there weren't plenty of biblical examples of men and women who never reached the pinnacle of success, whose lives mirrored perennial failure and hardship. We knew that Abraham had wandered around in the wilderness in tents all his life and that Stephen had been stoned to death. But many people explained those examples away. They belonged to another day—before the advent of American Express and lawyers with briefcases and power ties. Those models did not inform my great expectations because I had a filter in place.

Embarking on the Christian life, as it was oversold then and still is presented today, was like looking through a travel brochure for a tropical island vacation. Each four-color paged depicts a spread of inviting images, attractive accommodations, cheerful fellow passengers, and charming sights, all reasonably priced.

The actual excursion, though, is markedly different. There are detours and setbacks, and some much-anticipated events have been canceled altogether. And the price is greater than any of us imagined.[2]

Ted never envisioned the humbling process of having to ask his creditors to accept a modified schedule of repayment. When he heard other businessmen discuss the financial climate of his city, Ted expected that God would somehow protect him from feeling the full effect of the economic downturn. He knew he had a lot to learn about the floral business, but he hoped against hope that God would make up for his lack of knowledge.

Grant spent his early years as a Christian establishing all the right Christian habits. He regularly shared his faith with his unbelieving friends and rarely missed a day reading the Bible. All his life he had been the kind of person who did what he was supposed to do when he was supposed to do it. He believed that if he played by the rules, everyone else would as well, so he was unprepared for employees who fudged on the amount of vacation days they had taken or colleagues across town who made bold efforts to build their practices at the expense of everyone else's.

Susan had always believed that Christian spouses worked things out—they didn't divorce. Susan's image of herself was that of a supportive wife, a woman whose primary means of serving God was being a good wife and mother. She felt deeply defeated by her divorce. Learning what it meant to honor God and to trust Him in a role foreign to her thinking, that of a single parent, was an effort she had never expected to make.

It is in our thirties that such idealism starts to break down. In a decade marked for many people by mini-losses and letting go—when your job or your marriage or your illusions of personal grandeur wear thin—reality begins to replace the caricature.[3] We begin to grapple with life as it really is and to understand—often in retrospect—the illusions with which we began.

The Fallout

For those whose great expectations of life go hand in hand with great expectations of God, the fallout leaves a mark. The emotional residue can take longer to shake off than some of the original false notions themselves.

FALSE GUILT

One of the more common scars is false guilt—guilt when your life did not measure up, when after taking the tenth basic step to spiritual maturity you were still stumbling around. "I used to spend the best part of the weekend getting high on marijuana and cocaine until I became a Christian," says a budding college professor. "I think I tried Christianity like I would have tried a new drug. My friends had said, 'Try Jesus. Jesus can take you higher than cocaine.' I did. They were wrong."

In short order, that man decided that whoever came up with that idea had never tried cocaine. He gave himself a year or so, waded into all the spiritual activities and programs his friends said would make his life better, and then quietly began to do drugs again on the side.

He explains, "If that program I was following was supposed to alleviate any real struggles or problems I was experiencing, then I decided I must be doing the Christian life wrong. I felt like one big fake." The little dots of peace and gentleness and joy that were supposed to line up around the edge of his circle if Jesus was on the throne were, instead, dancing in stubborn disarray.

He admits that the guilt of not having his life completely together would have driven him back to drugs for good had he not met a few individuals who were better models of authenticity. They weren't captive to the notions that their struggles would disappear if they mastered the right spiritual techniques. He discovered that Jesus could take him higher, but only if he redefined "high."

"There must be something wrong with me." That is one of the easiest conclusions to draw when spirituality is cast in terms of the ability to transcend a difficulty, when there are "steps" and secrets" to a higher plane. If there are eight steps to moral freedom, for instance, and at the end of the eight you are still struggling with untamed lust, the guilt is enormous.

Where did we lose Martin Luther's description of the Christian life? It is not perpetual confidence but rather the process of a recovering drunk who climbs up on one side of the horse only to fall off the other side, get up and go at it again.

Larger-than-life expectations create their own kind of pressure. We cannot just be people-in-process. We must be fixed. So relates a man who tried to get rid of colitis for five years: "For a large part of my twenties," he explains, "I had this embarrassing physical problem that everybody knew came from anxiety and stress. It was like wearing a badge of spiritual defeat for me. I read every book, attended every seminar I could find, but little changed. Honestly, the guilt of not being together was worse than the disease."

FALSE PRETENSES

When the Christian faith is oversold or presented inaccurately, those who believe they are missing the secret go into hiding. Or at least they learn how to keep the messier parts of their lives well out of sight. It is ironic that a religion built on truth could be so used to foster pretense.

"For a long time I used to tell people how the grace of God had kept me from being deeply affected by my father's abandonment and my stepfather's abuse," one woman in her early thirties says. "I learned pretty quick what was and was not permissible to share. People wanted to see me as a collected, competent Christian, and I let them. The only problem was that I stayed stuck emotionally and spiritually right where I was. It took me years to muster the personal courage to get honest about my past."

A pastor relates that he always likened his early Christian experience to that of Cinderella living in a palace.[4] Much of the emotional turmoil and depression that resulted from growing up in an alcoholic family seemed to have evaporated. Later, however, the veneer began to get rough around the edges.

An unnerving level of personal defeat plagued him. Fears of dying and speaking in public (one as scary as the other) remained present in his life. How do you tell someone, if you're a pastor, that the thought of a pulpit is not unlike that of a coffin, that death and preaching are synonymous and filled with fear? "The more I kept my struggles a secret," he admits now, "the more phobic I became. Yet I held back from honest sharing because I felt that if I were only more godly, I wouldn't have these struggles in the first place." It took him a long time to realize the recurring struggles that made his life more like a battleground were simply a legitimate part of the Christian life.

Only when we realize that heaven is the place reserved for perfection and final completeness can we live without false pretense here on earth.

A FALSE CONTRACT

Perhaps every generation, in its own way, faces the temptation to reduce a faith full of mystery and ambiguity and wonder to something more manageable. It appears to be safer that way. As a result, we codify and concretize a God who insists on bursting our categories, who insists on surprising us.

The simplest way to box God in, so uncomplicated that we usually don't know we're doing it, is to fashion an unspoken contract with Him. It happens imperceptibly. Our newly acquired discipline and spiritual principles harden into the terms of a quiet bargain struck with God: our allegiance for His cooperation. We do this and God does that. In a crazy way, we think we can swap services.

While Ted watched his floral business flounder and struggled to meet his bills, he sat with a small group of Christians where someone talked about how he "had put God to the test and look how God had blessed." He found himself wanting to say, "So what do you do when you tithe and you work hard and you keep your priorities in order, and you are still losing money? If that works for everyone else, why not me?"

"My wife and I kept asking ourselves where we went wrong," he says. "I mean, had God led us into this business or not? We could only conclude that He had, in spite of all that had happened. But I think that, in a good sense, the experience finally moved us out of the of-course-God-is-going-to-bless-me realm."

It can be jolting when you first realize that God does not offer guarantees. Most of us don't realize the "terms" we have placed in our contracts until, in one way or another, they aren't met. Sometimes we don't know what our expectations are until they are not fulfilled. It's the empty spaces, the ones we didn't even know were there, that begin to hurt.

It is easy, for instance, to believe that the safety and warmth of a Christian environment offers protection and immunity from the disappointments in the world. One Midwestern wife explained that she and her husband had finished seminary with another couple, close friends with whom they hoped to begin a church planting venture in the Northwest.

"We were committed to the same philosophy and the same ideals, but much more than that, we were committed to each other as couples. We used to joke about how we would grow old together," she says.

They thought they understood each other's shortcomings, the scars they carried, their peculiar vulnerabilities. The church began to grown in a way that surpassed even their wildest expectations. One of the couples began to make some significant shifts in their philosophy of leadership. There seemed to be no way to resolve the growing differences between the two couples, and in order to preserve a single-minded approach, one couple had to leave and begin again, in another location.

How does this wife view her abrupt departure and the severing of such close relationships? "It sobered me up a ton," she explains. "I see how fragile we are as people, how much baggage we carry from our pasts. Before this, I always thought that, inside the body of Christ, God would somehow protect me from other people's failures." In other words, she became aware of her false expectation in hindsight, only when she realized it was not being met.

Many of us knew all along that pain and loss and struggle were part of the human condition, as common to the Christian as to the man on the street. But somehow, we thought that the way it affected us would be different. Says one man who is now the wiser, "I really thought that what I knew about God—my notebooks full of information, my spiritual expertise—would protect me from feeling the full force of the things I dreaded the most, things like failure and rejection and inadequacy."

Another woman looks back on years of infertility and four miscarriages. "It wasn't the suffering in this regard that surprised me," she says, but that "in my understanding of faith and the abundant life, rejoicing in the Lord and wading through grief were two incongruous concepts. I expected difficult circumstances, but I didn't expect to *feel* them emotionally in the same way any mother would. I thought somehow that God would let me live above the pain. But He didn't."

So it is that when we begin to release God from the contract He never signed, we take our first steps in learning what it means to *trust* Him. Years after our introduction to Christ, many of us have entered, as new initiates, the real rigors of spiritual growth; the slowly spun, weathered variety that comes only when you have taken your tenth basic step to Christian maturity and fallen down.

The principal means of going forward, in a personal and spiritual sense, becomes what we least expect—disappointment. It is a discovery that, even now, seems strange, like being led home by going abroad.

I believed that my life was on movable rollers and if I tried hard enough I could rearrange the pieces most any way I wanted.

Jay Larson, 34

5

Rude Awakenings

The End of Innocence

As we move from our twenties through the decade of our thirties, many of our youthful illusions become exposed to the harsh rays of real life. Heroes come down off their pedestals, the new and exciting settles into routine, we get saddled with responsibilities. The passage from youth to the advanced youth of middle age opens up exciting possibilities, but it contains its own series of subtractions as well—reminders not only of what we are becoming, but of what we might have been.

Often in the process of that passage, something unexpected happens that dislodges some of our most valued dreams, throwing us off balance. I call that "a rude awakening." It can take many forms—a death, an accident, a lost job, a broken relationship, an undesirable move, a dashed hope, a betrayal.[1] A rude awakening is closely akin to what Daniel Levinson, in his book about men's life stages, called a "culminating event," a circumstance that serves as a marker for the conclusion of young adulthood.[2]

A rude awakening, though, is not necessarily a monumental event. Other people might have negotiated that turn in the road as though it were only a slight detour. But for the person who is "rudely awakened," there is an inner sense of being stopped short, of wanting to ask, "Hey, what's going on here? My life is not unfolding the way I thought it would." It is as though a stray chapter from someone else's life had been thrown right into the middle of your own.

Stopped Short

It is strange how our lives can parallel the larger story of the times in which we have lived. One of the great figures of our childhood was John F. Kennedy. His Boston accent charmed us. His regal, princelike bearing made him an indelible hero, and Jackie in her pillbox hat added her own elegant touch.

Theodore White called the Kennedy years a "magic moment in history," when gallant men danced with beautiful women and great deeds were done, and the barbarians behind the gate were held back.[3] Even the later disclosures of Kennedy's less-than-noble tendency to court less-than-queenly women have not completely erased the aura of Camelot we associate with that time.

Those magical moments came to an abrupt end on a Dallas parkway in 1963. One moment the First Couple was waving to cheering crowds from the back seat of a black limousine, the next minute they were racing to a hospital. Jackie recounted that ride in utterly human terms: how she found herself struggling to put back the pieces of tissue that fell from the wound in her husband's head, as though the man in her lap was a doll that could be patched; as though the event itself could be rewound like a movie.

That picture of Jackie as the stunned widow, standing alone in her stiff pink coat, is a life-sized image of the sheer fragility of human experience. One minute life is moving ahead smoothly. The next, it appears to stand still.

Many of us have events, especially in our thirties, that though smaller in scale and of much less social consequence to be sure, markedly alter our direction or outlook.

For some, they are climactic; for others, simple, epiphanal moments. But surprises, disappointments, and tragedies divide our experience into small before and after categories. The earth was made round, says one African proverb, so that we would not see too far down the road. Or as John Lennon is often quoted, "Life is what happens while you are busy making other plans."

My own rude awakening began quite unexpectedly. My children were all in school and I was ready to move into some brand-new ventures. But one day I sat across from a doctor who told me point blank, with all the solemn finality of a minister's benediction, that I did not have the flu. I was pregnant. The queen of infertility, and I was pregnant.

I could not believe my ears. I left his office in a daze, clutching my abdomen as though it had a mind of its own and might suddenly decide to walk in the opposite direction. At home, the news of another baby was greeted with such excitement that I began to abandon my misgivings. "This is better than Christmas!" our daughter said as she ran off to measure whether her old doll bed would hold a real baby.

The longer I thought about a third child, the more inviting the prospect became. This time I could relax and *enjoy* a baby. There were four people—not two—waiting for the arrival of this child who, as weeks turned into months, became in my mind more and more "the perfect child," the one with the even-tempered disposition, who would learn to read at two.

I had known nothing but uneventful pregnancies, so I was doubly unprepared for the first wrenching pain and sudden gush of blood that mark the threat of miscarriage. I was pushing a cart in the grocery store parking lot when it happened. I went home and got into bed.

For days on end, I lay in bed. I read books, stared out the window, and prayed, hoping fervently that this life would survive inside me. But in those long hours it dawned on me that I had no control over whether I kept or lost this baby. For once, I had come up against something that I could not *will* to be different. I was powerless.

Strangely, my predicament brought to mind a game my son and I used to play when he was four years old and able to conjure up new worlds in his imagination with ease. First, he would gather the necessary articles of his life—his toy gun, his teddy bear, and a box of Cheez-Its—then he'd climb into a long clothes closet. After a while I'd hear him call, "Hey, Mom, come in here with me."

"Why, Brady? What do you want me in the closet for?" I'd answer.

"Because there are lions and tigers out there, Mom. And if you come in here with me, we can shoot them all—dead."

Having never been one to pass up truly important work, I would pile into his closet, find a less cluttered spot in a dark corner, and feed Cheez-Its to my young hunter as he fearlessly rid the bedroom of wild beasts. Finally, we would emerge, the triumphant pair.

My current bedroom scene was totally unlike that. How I wished I could dispense with real threats as easily as we had pretended to—I wished there were some human means of keeping the lions and tigers at bay.

Within a few weeks, I delivered a little boy one morning in the doctor's office. All his parts were miniature, skillfully-crafted, doll-like—and still. The obstetrician held up his tiny form and offered his condolence. I felt pathetically unprepared to say good-bye to this child as he lay cold and quiet atop a doctor's cabinet.

A few months later, after we had begun to absorb our loss, I was at the hospital visiting a friend when, with no warning, I rounded the corner of the newborn nursery. Instantly I took a deep breath. The sight of those babies, their cheeks plump and pink with life, took me back. This was the way babies were supposed to look. I shrunk from the contrast between their soft faces and the memory of that gaunt little boy with his eyes sealed shut.

Beyond the isolated incident of my miscarriage, I began to sense how carefully carved in my mind—and how many—were the images of how life ought to be. Careers without glitches, fellowship without friction, smart children who kept well-decorated rooms neat, and babies—especially babies—who nestled pink cheeks in warm receiving blankets. I never knew I had such a scripted picture.

Somehow I sensed, as only a woman can, that I would not be able to have another child. I could almost hear the door creaking shut. The memory of the child was a wrenching exit to the child-bearing years, a rending of my neatly arranged cosmos, my own personal rude awakening.

And the episode left me wondering what other stray calamities might come home to roost. I was now officially outside the protective bubble that I had been living in for years. I finally realized in a deep personal sense that my life was not a menu from which I was free to pick only the selections that suited my tastes.

Slow Dawnings

Not everyone likens this maturing process to a rude awakening. For some, there is no calamitous event. One day folds into the next, another deadline is met, and there is little time to reflect. Instead of rude awakenings, there are only slow dawnings. Little by little, you just sense your life evolving into something different than you imagined. Sometimes a feeling of stagnation, disequilibrium, or mild depression sets in. The results of earlier choices become plain, yet not easily reversed. Options seem to have narrowed, but responsibilities have grown.

The slow dawnings usually take place in our thirties, when we face up to our own personal "nevers." I will never be head of the firm or have children of my own or be rich and famous. However that "never" may present itself, it slowly dawns on us that we've been chasing a carrot on a stick.

It is sobering to realize that you may not be able to soar to the heights you once thought. "I had always thought of myself as a person with well above average abilities," says one woman, a middle-manager for a state agricultural agency. "But when I moved from Lincoln to Chicago I realized that there are a lot of talented people out there. I did well, but others were doing better. I grew up expecting to be discovered down at the corner drugstore, but more and more I suspect I will just plod along."

Those sentiments are echoed by many people in their thirties. It is a time of introspection, of critical self-evaluation. *Have I measured up? What would life be like now if I had made different choices? What changes can I make now?* Those kinds of questions speak of lost opportunities and hidden regrets, but they are necessary and may lead to midpoint changes of direction or corrections.

THE ILLUSION OF SUCCESS

Even those who have actually attained the goals they set for themselves experience an unexpected letdown. They've achieved what they thought they wanted, the fantasy gratified. The corner office. The book published. The brilliant baby. But it isn't enough—not for long. Something is still missing. The feeling of incompleteness stubbornly returns. Success is rarely all it's cracked up to be.

By the age of forty, Grant had reached his goal that had been ten years in the making, his fantasy gratified. He was finally able to open his own psychiatric practice on the outskirts of a large metropolitan city. It was what he'd gone to medical school for, the reason he'd paid his dues in another clinic and moved his family halfway around the country.

For the first year or so he felt the charge whenever he drove up to the building with his name out front. He enjoyed hiring staff that he believed could provide quality care. But, in fact, he had exchanged one set of problems for another. Some of the magical hopes he had attached to his dream evaporated in the never-ending string of "dailies." It wasn't as special as he thought.

A flat, hollow feeling, like soda pop when all the fizz is gone, began to plague him, the question *So what?* forming more often on his lips. Where was he supposed to go from here? What do you do for an encore? It was hard to admit the disappointment—the strange sense of deflation—he felt not upon the loss of a dream but upon realizing it.

What Grant found was the mirage-like quality of success. Euphoria is short-lived and not nearly as portable as we would like. Once we have struggled to the top of some mountain, another one appears that beckons us to climb again. There is always someone else who has done better, achieved more. One of the most ironic kinds of disappointment comes when we realize that outward success rarely changes inner realities. We can't fill up the empty spaces within by achieving even our biggest dreams.

THE ILLUSION OF CONTROL

Reckoning with old dreams forces us to face many of our false notions, one of which is the illusion that we are the master of our fate. That is the deceptive feeling that, if we're smart and stay on our toes, life will work the way we've planned. If we just try hard enough, we can stay in control. Somehow by piety, planning, or flint-faced determination we can keep our world intact. The M&Ms will melt in our mouths, not in our hands.

Rude awakenings or slow dawnings convince us, on an emotional level, of something else: sometimes there are forces at work that are much bigger than we are. We are not the master of our destiny. As one friend said of his dilemma, "I realized there was no human way possible that I was going to worm my way out of this thing."

In April of Ted's first year in the floral supply business, his accountant called to congratulate him. "Five years from now, you could own this firm outright," he said. "Keep up the good work."

One month later a former employee filed suit against Ted for letting him go. The employee won. Within a week one of Ted's three division managers told him she was leaving that day to work for a competitor. She took all her accounts with her. Then a string of customers went bankrupt on him—eight in one week.

Ted began to prepare for his July design show with more than usual energy. The once-a-year open house was the floral design school that Ted's business was known for all over town, the one-day affair that sparked his cash flow.

"Oh, God," Ted prayed, "if You could just let this open house do well."

But as Ted packed up the boxes at the end of the day, he didn't have to look at the computer printout to know it had been less than a success. He would be fortunate to break even. "It was at that point," Ted says, "that I realized I had come into a situation that was beyond my control. Nothing I did was working. Not even prayer. I saw how easily this business could slip through my fingers and I felt helpless."

Ted was expressing how it feels to be confronted with the limits of being human. The deceptive sense that we are in control of our own life fades, and what takes its place is the first stirrings of a healthy dependence on God and an appreciation of our need for other people.

THE ILLUSION OF EXEMPTION

Another false conception is similar to the illusion that we can control our own lives. We grow up with the idea that pain and heartache, evil and death, will remain outside the walls of our castle. Unexpected, unpleasant things happen to other people. But not us. Not now. And not this way.

Somewhere en route to maturity, that illusion starts to break down. We begin to personalize the theological reality of living in a renegade world. We realize our vulnerability. We start to understand that God never promised us immunity. Some of the effects of the fallen state of affairs will touch our lives, too.

When Susan discovered that she was developing the same arthritis that had plagued her mother all her life, she was frustrated and scared. But she was not upset. Everyone's life included some hardship, she reasoned.

When the structure of her marriage started to slip, though, that was another story. "I could not understand this transformation I saw taking place in Jim or the way our relationship was slowly degenerating before my eyes." She had been drawn to Jim's ability to think well and to put ideas together in ways that other people could grasp easily. There was a verse in Daniel that had always reminded her of Jim, that "light and understanding and wisdom" dwelt in him. That image became harder to reconcile with the man who felt the need, on occasion, to go out and get good and drunk after a hard day in the ministry. Obviously something was eating away at him. Eventually, he dropped out of seminary to go into business with his father.

"I remember one night," Susan recalls, "when we went out to dinner with some friends and Jim had too much to drink. He was out there in the middle of the floor going crazy dancing, and everyone was watching and laughing. But I felt like the man before me was dying; he sure wasn't the guy from Daniel. It broke my heart."

When Jim filed for divorce a year later and Susan took the girls and moved back home to Oregon, she was feeling desperate. Her life was out of control. "I had never doubted that, as Christians, we would have our share of problems," she says. "But we wouldn't divorce. It wouldn't happen to me."

"I didn't think that this could happen to me. How many times have we all asked those questions?

That's part of what makes the Bible such an inviting book, a book worth returning to when we are hit by the unexpected. Its comfort is found in its honesty. Even the way in which God orders the story contains a message. The Bible begins on a fundamentally positive note and ends in triumph, clean and sure; but between Genesis and Revelation, there are adulterous kings and reluctant prophets, and at least one woman too impatient to sit still for long. It's real life, not fairy tales.

That's encouraging. We can open the Book and find our lives on its pages. Mine is a normal Christian life—this one, with bills waiting to be paid and relationships in need of repair. It's not immunity we've been given, it's grace.

Christianity offers not a detour around trial and disillusionment but the courage to move through them.

Although our backgrounds may have given us a different impression, God never promised His children an escape hatch from pain. The rude awakenings and slow
dawnings that come with growing older invite us to un-
pack the heavy suitcase we've carried, the one filled with
our oversized dreams. We need a lighter load, less bur-
dened by unrealistic goals and false pictures of ourselves,
of crazy notions about what this life can deliver. It is an
utterly necessary discarding process.

Because faith in an illusion is the shakiest kind.

A Threshold to the Future

When a person is in the midst of facing up to and
letting go of old hopes, it is often difficult to see beyond
the immediate struggle at hand. The temptation is to level
out in resignation, tune out, and get mired in disillusionment. Walter Lippman is famous for saying that, though
we all grow older, it is by no means certain that we all
grow up. I think he meant that if we don't recognize the
transitional passage we are in, we often get stuck in it.

But if we take hold of our expectations and reel them
in a bit, we discover something unforseen. There is hidden
wealth in our disappointed dreams. We are offered an
"abundant life"; not the external, measurable, bigger and
better kind we once envisioned, but another one. We
stand on the threshold of a deeper sense of personal identity, renewed relationships, and a more realistic faith. Our
ideas about what constitutes the good life take on a different shape. Our own small contribution to the world starts
to seem big enough. A sense of renewal replaces the feeling of stagnation and decline.

This process starts on the inside and moves outward.
Growing up—really growing up—means that we grapple
with what's happening inside us, in our own private world

of relationships and expectations. When that internal work takes place, the real changes begin.

Most of these benefits are best understood when we observe the lives of people who once wrestled with disappointed ideals. And so we begin to look at their lives with a contemporary focus, exploring the way God has built and is building something better on top of the rubble of their crumbled dreams.

PART 3

THE HIDDEN WEALTH
IN
DISAPPOINTED DREAMS

I've bounced around for so many years as a mother, volunteer, schoolteacher, graduate student, and taxi driver that I no longer have much of an idea who I am.

Melinda Devoe, 40

6

Inner Spaces

The Search for Authenticity

W hen a significant aspect of a person's outer world is shaken, a quieter hidden process begins on the inside as well. Between the ages of thirty-five and forty-five, a shift in focus occurs and our attention is drawn to our own internal dynamics. Often that is precipitated by a disappointment that jars our sense of identity, of who we are.

But whatever the reason, the shift in focus is a God-given opportunity to take personal inventory of our lives. It is not meant to be a cul-de-sac of self-absorption; rather it is a chance to reassess, to sink our personal roots down into what is really true about ourselves, our relationships, our faith, our lives. It is as though God knew we needed the time to stand back and see ourselves from a larger perspective: What were our dreams, why were they so important to us, and where do we go from here? Sometimes that internal work takes the shape of a full-blown "identity crisis," a term that seems trendy until you find yourself in the middle of one.

The process of taking an inward look—my identity crisis—was the result of a dream that failed to materialize. In the mid-eighties my husband and I invested four years in launching a leadership institute at Glen Eyrie, the Colorado conference center for a Christian organization known as The Navigators. The work-study program attracted students from all over the U.S. and many other countries as well, and it consumed the energies of five staff couples who gave their full-time attention to the effort. We worked to provide the opportunity for intense spiritual and personal help in a warm environment, at a fraction of the cost of a traditional seminary. It was a good dream. But after four years we were forced to admit that it was not financially feasible to continue the program as it was constructed.

Those four years had required a heavy personal investment of me. Consequently, the change in plans deeply affected me. I found that when I could no longer hold onto the idealized image of myself as one half of a dynamic couple in ministry, I began to flounder. Who was I, then? I didn't know. For a while, I felt as if I had lost myself—a classic characteristic of an identity crisis. I came to associate those years with a word I loathed: *failure*. Although some wonderful things came from that time, we did not accomplish the goals we had set. And failure was another thing that, without having realized it, I believed that trusting God would save me *from*.

The middle passage of life is notorious for such inner wrestlings. It is the time when slightly balding men buy little red sports cars and mothers of small children feel the overpowering desire to have Ph.D.s attached to their names. This is when internal voices arise, posed as questions: What pushes me so hard? Why am I doing this day after day? Is it worth it? Why do I feel so alone? That is but a sampling of the questions raised. Discovering the answers is a process that takes us further along in our inner journey.

A Search for Authenticity

Perhaps the journey can best be described as a search for authenticity, for an identity that exists apart from anything we have accomplished or any of the roles we play.

The search for genuine identity is what Gerald May, the author of *Addiction and Grace,* calls an "underlying constancy of self." He says that we long to experience "some foundation of self that is invulnerable to any other experience, unaffected by anything else that might happen to us."[1] This pursuit, he says, is one that brings us to the center of what the Old Testament calls our heart. It is our real self, a sense of inner home, the place where we experience the closest, most direct contact with the presence of God.

In some ways we have been on this quest for identity all our lives. Underneath the veneer, the faint little question always flickers: Who am I, really? I am someone's wife, someone's mother, someone's teacher, someone's daughter—that much I know. But apart from what I do, who am I? Once I get beyond my string of achievements, past all the roles I play, *is anyone home?*

Actually, I am describing a universal question. You can hear it in the way Tolstoy likened one part of his own journey: "I felt that something had broken within me on which my life had always rested, that I had nothing left to hold on to."[2] He, too, had that floundering sense of emptiness that comes when some of the ways you've always used to define yourself no longer apply. Robert Frost talked of how his life had been a progression in which he lost enough to find himself.

For the postwar generation, our search for authenticity is expressed in more contemporary terms. Regardless of how it surfaces, though, the drive for a genuine sense of individuality has always been a powerful one for us.

A middle-aged father of three talks about how he knows who he is on paper and plastic. He only has to look in his wallet. There he finds his social security number, his company I.D., pictures of his children, and an array of credit cards. And then he says, half-jokingly, "Some days I wonder if I lost my credentials, could I prove that I exist?"

For Grant, the quest for authenticity became apparent when, in his thirties, he found himself missing his father, though the man had been dead for ten years. The relentless pressure of his life, the demands from all quarters, led him to wish his father was still alive. The load he was asked to shoulder as a husband, father, and employer left him longing to know his father as someone who could point the way.

"When I look back on our relationship now," Grant says, "I realize that there wasn't much friction between us. Mostly we just frittered away the time being cordial. Now, at this point in my life, I realize that coming to terms with myself as a man is directly related to the support and connection I should have experienced with the most significant man in my life—my father. Part of who I am is linked to who I was, and am, as this man's son."

Whenever we begin to ask questions about personal identity, we enter into a spiritual domain. We can see the answers reflected in the way that Jesus dealt with individuals. He looked behind Peter's "Simon facade" and told him that one day soon his identity as a stable, rocklike man (Cephas) would come to the fore.[3] Jesus reminded another of his disciples, Nathaniel, that He had known him before they ever met.[4] Nathaniel's innermost identity was held securely in the mind and heart of God.

So there is nothing essentially new or unusual about arriving at a point in your life where your focus shifts internally. An identity crisis, a search for authenticity, is primarily fueled by any or all of three factors: the process of growing older, a shifting self-image, or disappointment in others. All three are especially common to the era known as midlife.

Growing Older

The ordinary process of aging tends to strip us, to pare us down, to challenge our notions about ourselves. We are no longer the bright, young whiz kids with all the fresh ideas. We are beginning to slow down. Maybe the career that required so much prime time has already peaked and begun to recede as noticeably as your hairline.

Our children grow up before our eyes, and the laugh lines around those eyes turn into honest wrinkles. It is harder and harder to hold on to the illusion of being forever young. We aren't ready to party at 12:00 P.M.; now we're asleep by then. Columnist Dave Barry insists that one of the most traumatic aspects of turning forty is realizing that we no longer have the same body we had when we were twenty-one. "I know I don't," he writes. "Sometimes when I take a shower I look down at my body and I want to scream: 'Hey, THIS isn't my body! THIS body belongs to Willard Scott!'"[5]

New bulges appear in strange places, and as Judith Viorst says in her book *Necessary Losses,* we start "to inspire far less lust than we do respect. We're not quite prepared to settle for only respect."[6] She quotes from a wistful poem titled "The Age of Maturity":

> When I was young and miserable and pretty
> And poor, I'd wish
> What all girls wish: to have a husband,
> A house and children. Now that I'm old, my wish
> Is womanish:
> That the boy putting groceries in my car
> Sees me. It bewilders me that he doesn't see me.[7]

A future of endless possibilities no longer strings before us. Time is now being measured in terms of "How many years do I have left?" rather than chronological age. The process of aging breaks down some of our cherished images of self and challenges us to reach for a deeper, intransigent sense of identity. We now reach beyond appearances and address the question of substance. It is our chance to begin to offer others the whole of who we are and, in that offering, to discover a deeper level of personal authenticity.

Shifting Images of Self

The changes in youthful appearance and capacities, however, are not the only ones that force us to reevaluate ourselves. Our self-perception shifts in other ways as well, from an idealized self-image to a more accurate, balanced understanding.

Most of us spend the greatest portion of our lives fashioning an idealized image of ourselves—some version of a competent, pleasing personality that we feel comfortable presenting to an onlooking world. Early in life we learn to fine-tune our talents and how to offer what is required of us in order to be valued by others. We are heavily invested in our titles and advanced degrees, our individual expertise, and sharp presentations. Our strengths we know how to highlight, our weaknesses we have learned to hide. And in a convoluted way, our hope is that God is just as committed to keeping that idealized image intact.

The fear of exposure is all that holds that false identity in place. We are afraid that someone will peek behind that mask and discover an ordinary little boy or girl, unsure and overwhelmed by life, convinced that the only thing that provides worth is the abilities others find useful or commendable. "The fact that I could sing well enough to entertain or inspire people," one friend explained in her own metaphorical way, "became something of a screen I hid behind. It was like a coat two sizes too big that I hoped no one would peek through and laugh."

We learn how to play it safe; how to keep our real feelings, needs, and vulnerabilities so protected that, as the years go by, our real self is almost totally subsumed. We become plastic people, not the fully human, wonderfully alive beings God meant us to be, but experts in pretending—strangers, even to ourselves.

Fortunate are those for whom setbacks or a new development challenges that idealized self-image. That is part of what Ted experienced when his business slid into deep financial strain. He had always been the kind of guy others looked to for advice. He stood out in a crowd as a natural leader, a model of integrity and good business sense. He was the one always asked to give workshops or gather a men's group for weekly breakfasts.

"I had built my life around my idea of what an accomplished Christian businessman looked like," Ted says. "This was the image I groomed myself for, the person I felt God intended me to be."

But when his business encountered financial difficulties, Ted began to take the backseat. People were not looking to him for much of anything. For the first time, he was in a men's group of business owners, and he didn't lead the group. He said little. He thought he had nothing to share.

The group was led by a younger man, a new Christian for whom everything was going beautifully. "This guy would make a move," Ted recalls, "and God would bless him hand over fist. He came out of his contract negotiations with stuff I'd never heard of." It was hard to watch others do so well without concluding that his own problems were a commentary on his own failures.

Ted had always prided himself on being able to meet his financial obligations as they arose. "I think my lowest point," he says, "was when I had to call a Jewish supplier who knew I was a practicing Christian and ask him to help us work out our payments on time. Later, as I realized how many people who owed me money were refusing to even return my phone calls, I saw that my candidness was an opportunity to show some character."

At the time, though, Ted felt humbled to the core. Struggling with his business had a way of stripping away everything he thought he had—his abilities and strengths, his concept of himself as the young, successful go-getter.

Though it felt as if his outer skin were being peeled away, and though he fought the urge to cover up the pain, Ted recognizes that this dismantling process left him in a better position than he realized. "I became a lot more honest about myself. It's hard to hide your weakness and your pain when you are stretched to your limits. I feel like I emerged as more of a whole person—a human being rather than a performing artist. What I have to give people now—who I am—flows as much from my failures as it ever did my success."

When we are forced to reach beneath our idealized self-image, we discover that there is an average, ordinary person there; one with needs and feelings, with particular opinions and longings. Beneath our polished appearance exists a real person who was embraced at the cross, a son or daughter of God with an innate identity that could never be earned, only claimed. A. W. Tozer once said that because God thundered from the heavens, "I AM," we were enabled to answer back in feeble but authentic voices, "I am, too." There really is someone home.

Disappointment in Others

We live in the context of relationships—with friends and mentors, spouses and parents—and invariably, we invest much of who we are in our trust and dependence on them. When someone fails us, the way we view ourselves is often deeply shaken.

As a generation, we have never been in short supply of heroes. We have a long history of attaching our personal hopes and dreams to mythic figures such as Martin Luther King, Jr., or Robert Kennedy. Looking up to people, believing that what they said was what they meant, came naturally to us for the longest time. When that faith was broken, through death—as in King's and Kennedy's case—or through the discovery that many of our heroes had feet of clay, disillusionment set in. Our dreams and the picture of where we fit into them had to be reevaluated.

A similar process takes place in the arena of close relationships, but the disappointment when someone close leaves you hanging high and dry is much more profound. I spoke with an import-export entrepreneur, a man in his late thirties who told me that his greatest disappointment centered on a mentoring relationship with a man in his church. "This guy led me to Christ in his youth group," he said, "and over the years he became a kind of father figure to me, a man of integrity I could take my cues from."

My friend watched that man's influence in the business world grow to national and international stature, and he began to follow in his footsteps. "That's why I found it a bit ironic," he relates, "to have been on an overseas trip when I heard that this man had been having an affair with a woman in the church. I felt let down, as though maybe this man's failure had invalidated a lot of my own life as well as his. I remember turning to my wife and telling her that somehow it all made my own achievements seem stale. It stole some of the joy."

What my friend was voicing was a disappointment born of the fear of being left on your own. Suddenly the hero spot is empty. A parent has died, or is lapsing into second childhood, and is no longer there to be leaned on. Instead, he is leaning on you. Or our parents don't retire to Florida the way they're supposed to; they divorce and flounder solo. Or the friend you always admired seems to turn on you. Somehow, it feels as though there is no one out front, and yet there may not be enough support around you and you are forced, finally, to learn what it means to gather strength from within. You reach for the part of you that is not fused with the success or failure, the faithfulness or unfaithfulness, of anyone else around you.

Letting go of our dependencies can be painful because they are what protect us from that raw sense of feeling alone. And alone can be an awful way to feel. As long as I can idealize someone by lionizing his strengths and overlooking his humanness, I will never have to face the need to find my own rightful strength. To face someone else's limitations is also to admit my own—and to be left feeling alone and dependent on God in a whole new way.

. I think of how I usually prefer to ride the waves when we are at the ocean with our children. I rarely choose to face such big, unknown waters without first grabbing one of the kids' rafts. The ocean is still a strange place to a woman who's more at home in the mountains. You never know what creatures lurk beneath all that foam and spray. And in some childish part of my brain, I still think that the crabs won't bite my toes and the jellyfish won't sting me—

as long as I'm holding on to that raft. I find it as hard to walk into the ocean standing on my own two feet as I do to move forward in life without leaning on another person to keep me safe.

The closer the bond between two people, the harder the blow when one of them deserts or disappoints the other, and the more we struggle with questions about our own identity. Susan remembers her sense of grief as she watched the image of the man she knew as Jim begin to unravel. "I knew this guy had so much to offer, an intensity and strength I found hard to describe," she says. "But there was a darker side, too, with wild mood swings and unpredictable anger. That was the part I had never let myself admit, until it was too late."

It took Jim's leaving to bring Susan to the point where she started to ask the personal questions she should have asked much earlier. For the longest time after he left she was numb, vacant, unconnected. Then she began to feel as if she'd been robbed. She says, "I realized that I had only given Jim the parts of myself that I felt he wanted. He had taken that, but somehow I always knew that I never satisfied him."

She had done whatever it took to please him, doling herself out in little bits until it seemed that there was nothing left. She felt "invisible" even to herself. People asked her what she wanted to do now. Where did she want to go from here? Susan had no idea.

"It was then," she says, "that I saw I had lived like a chameleon all my life. It wasn't just with Jim. I had been a mirror that reflected whatever color or shape was put before it. When Jim was no longer available to lean on, I was forced to discover who was the 'I' that had been absorbed by the 'we.'"

So it is that once our bubbles begin to burst, our trusted notions about ourselves and those we love start to fade, and we begin to take a deeper look at who we really are. The journey is a rite of passage in the mysterious thing called "growing up."

It is a new beginning in a personal and spiritual sense—a fresh start at taking the small, wobbly steps of learning to stand on your own two feet.

I got tired of imitation margarine and fake fur. I got tired of synthetic fabric and man-made snow and wearing a toupee. But most of all, I got tired of an imitation me.

Ronald Castle, 36

7

Becoming Real

Growing Up from the Inside Out

When actress Glenn Close was given an honorary degree by her alma mater, The College of William and Mary, she was also asked to give the commencement address in place of George Bush, who politely declined.

She admits that for a long time she had no idea what she would say when it came time to speak. She had only been asked to speak in the first place, she realized, because as an actress, she had excelled at the difficult art of pretending to be someone else, to say someone else's lines.

She could remember each of the characters she had played, and immediately the words they would have said would form on her lips. She knew which would have shown herself to be politically astute and well informed, which never would have been asked, and which would have declined quickly as she received the invitation.

But who am I? And what can I say? she asked herself.

Despite her self-doubt, she went on to give a superb commencement address filled with the insight she had gained from her childhood, in the theater, and from the support of various friends and mentors. When you read her speech, you realize that she had in her own mind and heart the words she needed all along.

As Glenn Close gave that commencement address where she played herself, she mirrored the developmental challenge we all face. At some point we must learn what it means to speak our own lines. The process of growing older, of facing the disappointments that jar our sense of identity, is one of discovering the role we are called to play and gathering the courage to let go of the masks we have hidden behind. We begin to play our own role and to own our own life.

We are not alone in facing that challenge. The question of individuality, of personal authenticity, is at the heart of what it means to follow Jesus. Here was a man who resisted the temptation to be anyone other than who He truly was, the Son of God. He refused to be made into a political reformer or a leader of the Jewish liberation from Rome, to put on any other than His true identity as the Messiah. So when we set out to follow Him, we embrace one who is committed to bringing us into a life built on honesty and lack of pretense, where what we experience is an ever-increasing freedom to be the person God had in mind when He created us.

We need to be aware, however, that this process contains no basic steps that insure a sense of mastery and performance. There is no "how-to" formula that brings us into a solid sense of personal identity. That is why it is best likened to an inner journey, one that is individualized and unpredictable, and over which we have little control. There are no shortcuts to avoid the confusion and emptiness. Instead, the route wanders and meanders and only reveals how far you've come in a few scenic spots.

Growing up means integrating the past and the present with new possibilities for the future, embracing the lost, abandoned parts of ourselves we have orphaned along the way. Perhaps somewhere, without realizing it, we turned our back on the person we wanted to be all along.

"I hate to admit that I am thirty-eight years old and

only now beginning to realize that my goals were never my goals." So begins a man who spent years in the career field he was "expected" to enter and now, finally, is halfway through a graduate program that will prepare him to teach. "Sometimes I get angry," he says, "that I have spent so many years on automatic pilot, headed toward the idea of being this great businessman, only to discover that was never me."

He always had tunnel vision for that goal, doodling around in school, convinced that one day he would take over his father's manufacturing franchise. The business had consumed his father's energy, and he grew up never questioning that he would someday follow in his father's steps.

Now, with a better-late-than-never attitude, he is starting to detach himself from that goal. "I tried so hard to fit for so long, to be interested in the things that businessmen are interested in. Now that I'm away from that world I find I don't even look at the business section in the newspaper," he says.

Instead, he finds that he enjoys academic life; the inquisitive world of the college professor is a much closer match to his own reflective nature. "I wish I had understood who I was when I was twenty-five, but I didn't," he adds, "I'm just thankful to be coming into my own now. I think I might have gone on forever just trying to be my father's son, never having lived my own life."

For the person willing to wade through the struggle of letting go of old dreams, willing to take a closer look, the process starts to look more like an inviting opportunity. He begins to sense that "Yes, there is something happening in here. And it's starting to feel pretty good."

When you're in the middle of this journey, it is natural to ask where you are going. What comes to the person willing to tramp around in the backwoods of self-questioning? Some very encouraging things, it turns out. There is a hidden fortune in disappointment when it forces you to take a closer look at who you are.

The Freedom to Live Within Your Limits

One of the most recognizable changes is a new ability to live within your limitations. The pressure to be good at everything—to be *omnicompetent*—may be replaced by the quieter contentment of making your own particular contribution. Many describe it as a new freedom—a release from the lifelong urge to please, to fill in the gaps of everyone else's expectations.

That is no small feat, though, particularly for our generation. Our congenital weakness for great expectations and big dreams is that much of those demands were focused squarely on our *selves*. We were supposed to cure cancer within our lifetime and write an end to poverty. We were the first to attempt the amazing task of trying to be two sexes at once. No one who had braces and a college education paid for could be merely average, right?

The sheer pace of life alone pushes us to adopt a superhuman capacity. We race out the door to work in the morning, driven men and harried women with hurried children. Many hours later, after a quick Clark Kent change of costumes, we become homework supervisor or the congenial host or innovative lover or a combination of all three, until we collapse for the night, wearied and worn—ready to get up and do it all again tomorrow.

Is it any wonder that we feel pressure, the great, pounding internal pressure, to be more than who we are? Or something different from what we are?

The situation for Christians is even more demanding. Our expectations are often a cross between John Wayne and the apostle Paul. The spiritual rationale of omnicompetence goes like this: "The same God who created microscopic amoebas and flung the stars into space also lives in me. I can, therefore, do whatever needs to be done. If I exercise enough faith and willpower, God will enable me to meet whatever needs arise." When we embrace that illusion, however, His voice is mistaken for another one among many, all pushing us to overdo, to live beyond our limits.

One businessman who lives in the glitzy hyperbole of Dallas spoke of how he learned, the hard way, that he was not superhuman. "I had lived for years," he says, "feeling like Atlas trying to hold up the world on my shoulders. Being a Christian somehow got all mixed up with that, and before long, I simply added a horde of Christian activities to the load I was already carrying."

He began to meet with a group of men on Saturday mornings for study and encouragement, only to find himself being nibbled away by envy. After all, it was Dallas. "I got tired of parking my decrepit Volkswagen behind those guys' BMWs," he says, "so I just made up my mind to double my efforts at work." He also became an elder in his church and led dozens of men's groups, all the while straining to be a model husband and father.

Eventually, he developed a bleeding ulcer. Four days in the hospital and a month's forced rest gave him some perspective. What he realized is what many of us discern when we reach midlife's burial ground and see for ourselves the gravemarkers of our impossible personal expectations.

"I came to grips with the fact that I was only good at a few things," he says. "Some guys are always going to have more than I do, and that's OK. The spiritual life is not a one-man show. God has put me on a team." He now sees himself as a Barnabas who affirms other people's contributions, while specializing in what he's really good at—relating to non-Christians. He learned to say, "That's enough, and that's OK."

THAT'S ENOUGH, AND THAT'S OK

What magical words of freedom those are. We experience an inner release when we let go of those inflated illusions of ourselves. Like the Dallas businessman, we can major on a few things that grow out of the center of who we are and let the superfluous go. That requires the courage to say no more often, to let go of the call-me-for-anything role we so easily slip into. Our sanity is restored to the measure that we discover our niche and capitalize on that.

Living with your limits, being able to say, "That's enough, and that's OK," does require faith, but faith of a whole different sort. When we begin to recognize our gifts and inherent temperament, our best sphere of influence, we are, in fact, exercising faith in the thoughtful pattern in which God made each individual. We contribute to the whole as specialists in only a few things, learning to live in the humility of our God-given limitations.

"For years, I was shooting for a composite ideal which was really the best traits of two or three people I admired all rolled into one," explains one woman. "I just kept plugging along toward that goal, working to shore up my weak points, hoping to emerge as the phantom woman." When she finally realized, in her late thirties, that she wasn't reaching her goal, she began to take a closer look at her own identity. "I finally realized that I have an inherent set of abilities and interests, and that I can only be what I am." The faith she exercises now is the faith to become fully who she is, the woman God made her to be. She is finally able to say, "That's enough, and that's OK," and mean it.

ACCEPTING LIMITATIONS

When we do begin to exercise that kind of faith, there are implications. Living within your limitations means accepting how high, or how far, those limitations can take you. People who know the freedom to be themselves are people who have brought their dreams into line with reality and feel at home there.

Sometimes lowering your sights is painful, as one woman who had invested years in the dream of being a well-known writer knows. For a long time it looked as though she might realize her hopes. She had finished the largest part of four books in record time and appeared on a national television program that the producer called "a perfect show."

Then in the course of ghost-writing a book for a pair of husband-wife concert pianists, she happened to visit them in their home. "All of a sudden, I realized what real success in a professional field looks like," she says. "I listened to their phone ring at all hours for bookings. I watched their video, and I saw firsthand the kind of promotional backing a publisher was willing to give their book."

With a jolt, she knew that anything she had done was small potatoes in comparison. She was not ever going to be a "star"; she was simply a good utility writer who could capture someone else's story on paper. That was as far as her talent and life circumstances would take her.

For a while she floundered, feeling as if the train had left without her. She was back at the depot in a small Midwestern town, with a husband who sold insurance and two kids who needed rides to swim practice. "Well, all right," she said, "I guess this is it." Then she began to take a fresh look at what "it" was. She and her husband began to reforge the connections they had lost while she was buried behind the computer. She carved out the space to breathe, to ride bikes with the kids, to read more books for pleasure.

"Once I stopped pushing to achieve the impossible," she says, "then my efforts weren't so weighted with the need to prove myself. Writing is much more enjoyable when you don't have to become the star of stage and screen or change all of Western civilization. I was free to enjoy the rippling effect of the impact I was having." She could walk into a bookstore and see the book she had ghost-written for someone else and think, *Hundreds of people will read these words, and it's OK that my name isn't plastered on the pages.* "I found that I could have more if I was willing to settle for a little less."

A New Capacity for Intimacy

Another benefit of facing your identity questions head-on is a deeper ability to love others. The reason is this: When we are uncomfortable with who we are, when our emotional survival depends on keeping our idealized image intact, we are not free to love. Our energies are siphoned off by the task of protecting that image. We peek around at each other from behind a thousand masks, trying to escape the risk of letting someone into the inner circle of our lives.[1]

When I am afraid to let another come close, afraid that she will leave if she knows my life is less than perfect, the only emotional choice is to distance myself from everyone who appears to have the power to cut me down to size. The prospect of intimacy feels like a dance in the dark, full of awkward moments of trying to avoid the pain of having one's toes stepped on. Everything becomes tighter, more rigid and constricting, brittle to the emotional touch. We are cut off from what we were made for, that is, to love well and to be loved in return.

God created us with a longing for intimacy that no amount of super achieving can satisfy. The more we come to peace with ourselves as God made us, the more free we are to enjoy the intimacy for which we were made. The energy we used in the past to live defensively is channeled, instead, into someone else's life. We are no longer running scared, afraid of being exposed in the painful way we have worked so hard to avoid.

When some stray calamity jolts us enough to make us drop our masks, a whole new world of relationships becomes possible. That's why a true inner journey always comes full circle. An inner journey includes outward movement as well.

That is why Ted, in some ways, views his business difficulties as a liberating experience. They challenged his perceptions of himself and freed him to enjoy relationships. The overwhelming nature of his financial problems forced him to admit he was not in control. For once, he was the one who needed advice and consolation. "I began to discover that when I was with a friend," he says, "I was no longer working double-time trying to keep up my great image. It suddenly seemed pointless not to share with him the reality of what I was up against." A healthy sense of reciprocity began to characterize some of his closer friendships.

"As a result of that time I see more of what it means to be totally present with someone," Ted says. "I can enjoy them with a kind of self-forgetfulness that comes from not having to defend myself or my ideas. I can hear what they are saying to me without getting my hackles up, and I can offer them the same honest ear." There is an inner ease that seeps into our relationships when we are not living in a state of vigilance, forever on guard to protect a fragile inner ego.

An Inner Resilience

Thus, questions about identity foster inner freedom and a greater capacity for intimacy. Yet there is another benefit even more fundamental. We begin to discover an inner resilience we did not know we possessed.

As long as we can keep our life moving forward the way we hoped it would, we never have to confront our fears. Paradoxically, that avoidance only allows the anxiety to grow. If life never delivers us a blow so fierce that we are knocked off our feet, we will never know if we are strong enough to get up again. There is no way to grow strong in the broken places, as Hemingway described them, no way for God to meet us at our point of need. We never get the chance to face some of our fears head-on and stare them down.

Susan describes this process as "confronting the bogeyman." Being forced to play the role of a single parent was, for her, such an undesirable prospect that she never let herself consider the possibility—until she had to. And although she would never have chosen that situation, she nevertheless feels the bittersweet satisfaction of having confronted her worst fears and survived.

"I feel like someone who lived through a terrible automobile crash. I not only made it; in some important ways, I overcame," she says. As a result, she finds that she no longer rides as tight, braced for some imaginary disaster to come crashing down on her head, afraid that she will be swept away by something too devastating to handle.

There is enormous pleasure in touching bottom and finding it more solid that you thought. Ted, too, sees the hidden success in his business struggles: "Sometimes I feel like the Velveteen Rabbit. The difference in me now and five years ago is that I've had just enough of the threads rubbed bare and the seams stretched out of shape to know I'm real. I know what it is to survive and even profit by a situation that I thought for sure would do me in."

The inner resilience evidenced in Susan's and Ted's lives is the result of laying hold—in an emotional, experiential way—of a sense of the invincibility of your soul. Here beneath your fear is your most essential self, the innermost identity that the apostle Peter declared was "protected by the power of God" from now through all eternity.[2] This is your soul, your identity which required the death of Jesus to secure. No matter what adversity you encounter, you stand fundamentally protected because God has pledged Himself to your preservation. The dismantling of your ego's superstructure brings you to the indestructible essence of your own soul.

Disappointment can lead to inner wholeness because it gives our emotions the opportunity to integrate with our mind. One man from the Midwest whose divorce had shattered his world related how it opened up the whole emotional side of life for him. "I grew up on a farm," he explains, "where work and production were the big deals. As kids, we raised 4-H calves—slept with them and played with them—but when the fair came you hoped they won the blue ribbon because then you'd get a dollar a pound for the meat instead of 10 cents. Things lived and died and you learned to grow callous to the process. That was just life. You didn't waste time on feeling anything."

A few years after his divorce, though, a friend pointed out to him that he was bitter, angry, even grief-stricken. How could that be? He didn't see himself that way. He didn't even have a frame of reference for any of those emotions. He knew that God promised to bind up the brokenhearted and to heal the wounded spirit, but it took him a long time to see that those promises could apply to him. "I began to realize that you have to know that you're brokenhearted before you can experience any healing. Allowing yourself to feel, as well as to think and choose, is part of becoming a whole person."

Part of that inner resilience comes from the satisfaction of recognizing that pain and loss are intractable aspects of life. It means that you don't have to expend all your energy trying to avoid the unavoidable. Through disappointment you acquire the tools to deal with losses. You can feel the pain, and when the time comes, you can leave it behind and go on. You can live on the dark and the light side of life and gather the richness from both. You experience wholeness.

Without failure or disappointment, we would avoid facing our own neediness, and God would remain only a distant acquaintance. But having confronted that inner emptiness, every loss or disappointment becomes a hollow spot, a room in our own inn where God is invited, once again, to be at home. That is how our disappointments actually service our faith—these are the places where we sense God stirring in the deeply personal issues of our lives.

How like Dorothy in the *Wizard of Oz* we are. We set off on the impossible journey of returning to the place where we belong, to our roots in Kansas. Somewhere en route, in the strangest places, we discover our own heart and mind and courage. Like Dorothy in her ruby red slippers, we find that we have been given what we needed all along to make this trip. It is ourselves that we uncover, the indestructible part of our soul held securely in the mind and heart of God.

That is part of the mystery, I think, in discovering more of who you are. At the same time that you are coming home to yourself, you are coming home to God. It's not simply that the porch light has been left on to disguise a dark, vacant house. There really is someone home.

I can program a computer and design an auditing system for my company's accounts. I can cook a mean plate of Italian pasta. I even bake my own bread. But I don't do relationships very well at all.

Mary Whittaker, 34

8
Loose Connections
Intimacy at the Crossroads

Love is all we need," sang Mel Carter in 1966, and we sang along with him. If love was what was needed to make a relationship work, we thought we had enough to go around. We were the generation for whom equality and honest communication and getting-in-touch-with-your-feelings were supposed to break down the barriers to creating truly optimum relationships.

Unlike our parents who managed to place a man on the moon, we turned to conquer a different geography altogether; perhaps one that was even more treacherous. We set out to shorten the distance between each other.

Close friendships, transparent relationships, deep conversations. We have sifted through a wide variety of phrases that all speak of the same goal—intimacy. Over the years we have cohabited and interfaced, committed too seldom or loved too much. Now, who can draw a clear picture of "the perfect relationship"?

It all looked so easy in the beginning. If we could focus national attention on an unpopular war and racial equality, then establishing close connections between each other should have been a simple task. We thought we had relationships all figured out. Then we actually got into one.

The relationship that naturally held the focus of our greatest expectations was marriage. In the liaison between a man and a woman countless dreams and plans and prayers have been centered. What more obvious place to hope for intimacy than between two people who promise to share heart and soul, bed and bank accounts for a lifetime? And what more difficult?

In that most intimate of connections, the riddle of the gulfs between individuals is clearly depicted. At times they are small, like the space between two clasped hands during a lovers' stroll on a deserted beach. At other points, you could leap across a canyon easier than walk across a room and gather that familiar form into your arms.

Our generation has tried hard to improve on our parents' notion of husband and wife, marriage and family. "Married partners once settled for duty, but today's mates expect to be ecstatic lovers, intellectual colleagues, and partners in tennis and water sports," says professor of psychology Martin Seligman. "We even expect our partners to be loving parents, a historical peculiarity to anyone versed in the Victorian child-rearing model."[1]

Many of us saw our parents divorce or separate or just stand there paralyzed, unable to move toward each other in any meaningful way. We expected to do better. Here too, in the arena of relationships, we often wedded our expectations to our faith. "I thought that because my wife and I were two committed Christians and felt God had His hand in our relationship," explains a telephone salesman from Houston, "ours would start out like we'd been married for forty years. It would be a little slice of heaven on earth, and it wouldn't even *resemble* what my parents had." He is quick to admit, however, that though Christian principles have come to their aid, he and his wife have faced impasses they never expected.

Harder Than We Thought

So creating relationships that thrive, rather than merely endure, for a lifetime has been harder than we thought. Love may have been all we needed, but love can be pretty hard to come by. A couple who began by feeling they owed each other "the sunshine in the morning" may feel years later that they are just passing each other in the dark. By the time they pay the mortgage, educate their children, and coach Little League, there is little time left for each other.

One reason we find the task of creating intimacy such a challenge is that we bring so much baggage from our checkered pasts into our present relationships. "I have to admit that I was dismayed to see what was really required to make a relationship work," says a man approaching forty as he looks back over fifteen years of marriage. He grew up in a series of three homes with a mother who kept moving on to the next husband. "Throughout my thirties I always had the feeling that I would stick with my wife until I found this phantom woman who could give me the life I wanted," he says. "I didn't know what that was, but it was symbolized by that woman out there, somewhere." Though he didn't leave his wife, his anger and restlessness took a toll on their marriage. Not until he saw that he could not use his present relationship to make up for the deficit of the past was he able to begin to establish a solid basis for intimacy with his wife.

Building genuine intimacy is no simple task, even when a person knows how to do it. As a psychiatrist, Grant spends the best part of his day wading in and out of people problems—especially relationship breakdowns. And although he offers his advice and counsel all through the day, it is another thing entirely to create the needed dynamics in the context of his own marriage.

Only recently has he begun to see that the emotional detachment so necessary for his work environment is a detriment at home. There it easily becomes a protective layer that even his wife cannot get through. He realizes that her depression is not only the result of a difficult pregnancy and childbirth. It has to do with her past—and with him.

"I've begun to apply more of my own tonic," Grant explains. He has scaled back some of his professional commitments in order to give his own marriage more attention. "My wife and I aren't part of some mythical group of untroubled people with no problems to sort through. What I've learned from watching and trying to help other people with their relationships, I am beginning to use more right here at home."

Intimacy is an elusive goal in any relationship, not something that happens automatically just because we want it. It seems, sometimes, that the closer you get to another person, the more clearly you see the real obstacles and issues that keep you apart. Whether a friend or spouse, parent or child, we call to each other "across the incalculable gulfs that separate us."[2]

Forging New Connections

The middle years of life are one place where those "incalculable gulfs" become particularly apparent. That can be a challenging time in any relationship, because the unresolved issues usually become more evident as a couple nears the years around forty. Women in their late thirties are especially susceptible to feelings of loneliness, even in marriage—relational estrangement that may be called "feeling alone together."[3]

Another reason midlife can produce stress in a relationship is that it is when men and women each experience a drop in hormone levels, with differing responses. When a woman realizes she has had her last child, she begins to look harder outside the nest for places to channel her energy and drive. Emotionally and physically, she is ready to take on the world. Often that new confidence and motivation coincide with an opposite response in her husband. He has been making his way through the asphalt jungle for years. Just about the time his wife is gearing up to take flight, his thoughts are turning toward home, toward an admission of his own relational needs.[4]

In other words, the rhythms of their achieving and nurturing drives are out of sync. They may miss each other totally, each becoming an obstacle in the other's path. But, hopefully, they will meet on a whole new level of understanding and support. Forging new and deeper connections is a common task for couples at this stage in life. For many, the time seems ripe for change.

From our earliest days, Stacy and I had quietly prided ourselves in how much we could accomplish as a couple. We were both hard drivers, two workhorses yoked together in a common cause. Because it was so important to move full steam ahead, we learned how to avoid messy scenes between us, especially emotional ones. We learned how *not* to need each other too badly. The tears, the arguments, the drawn-out discussions tend to slow a person down. We agreed, in the tacit, unspoken way that couples do, that we simply did not have the time for that.

If ever a hint arose that something might get out of hand, I pulled the old writer's trick. "Let's stop talking here," I would say to Stacy. "It's obvious that this is upsetting us both. I'll just write out the way I see this situation so you'll have the benefit of my objective perspective." So I would write up my thoughts like a lawyer's brief, carefully deleting any potentially emotional word from the text.

The problem came when I awoke one summer in disturbing discontent. Something was missing between us, something I couldn't even put into words. I admired Stacy's talents, but more and more he just seemed like a familiar old friend whom I lived with. I couldn't *feel* much of anything.

If we had come together to accomplish a common task, we had succeeded admirably. If marriage was a goal, rather than a relationship, we had met the requirements.

We enjoyed many of the same pursuits and our values were remarkably similar. But somewhere in all our busyness, we had let the emotional connections between us go. It was the matters of the heart, the essence of our relationship, that we had both neglected. After almost twenty years of marriage we sensed that we had begun to drift apart and that it was time to take a hard look at the reasons why.

This stage in life may be especially designed by God to force that kind of reflection. The gap between the great hopes of our past and the hard realities of the present motivates the soul searching that brings about real change and personal growth. We have the potential to forge new connections through a variety of means, but three in particular play a significant role.

CONFRONTING OUR FEAR OF INTIMACY

The challenge of intimacy can best be likened to what it's like to talk, to kiss, to connect with someone through thermopane glass. In a close relationship there is a translucent wall through which you can see and hear and watch the other person, but only on rare occasions are you able to actually break through the barrier and really touch.

The reason that real intimacy is so difficult is that the closer we come together, the deeper we are taken into the territory of our own worst fears. Love, if it's real, can always be rejected, and the possibility of rejection or ridicule from a person who matters to us is not a pleasant one. Ambivalence sets in. On one level, the prospect of intimacy entices and woos us. Yet on a deeper level, fear begs us to play it safe. Instinctively we know that intimacy demands a high price because of the effort and risk involved in being that vulnerable.

In nearly every case, though, those risks are the very ones we need to take. When Stacy and I began to open our lives to each other on a deeper level, our actions were exactly counter to the safe habits we had spent years perfecting in order to keep our distance. All of a sudden the rules were changing, and we were both thrown off balance. We learned to lean less on sheer logic and to trust, instead, our instincts and intuition. It took determination to face the times when we had let each other down, and time to get honest about what was really bothering us. We had our share of messy scenes with no carefully worded lawyer's brief to cushion them. And somewhere in the midst of it all, we forged new connections that reminded us again of the reasons we married each other in the first place.

When breakthroughs like that occur, new life is brought to the relationship. Slowly you make connections in the very places where harm has been done in the past.

LINKING ARMS

Midlife can mean the chance to pull together against all the odds that would normally defeat you. Aging parents, resistant teenagers, a struggling business—the stress can drive you closer together and move you beyond a simple I-do-this-you-do-that kind of relationship. This is one of the insights that Ted and his wife, Anne, discovered as they combined their efforts to make a go of their floral distribution business.

At first, the fact that they were partners in a business as well as a marriage seemed as much of a problem as a blessing. Ted always dealt with the clients and managed a sale and supply team of twelve employees. Anne, who was an artistic person by nature, helped him create a display room with more style and flair than any other supplier in town. But she also knew the state of his accounts receivable.

When the business first took a downward turn, they spent hours discussing how they should respond—planning new initiatives, figuring out what they could do without, second guessing their decision to start the business in the first place.

As the weeks turned into months, though, and the downward turn became a sinking spiral, they talked less and less. "We just seemed to leave each other with more worry than when we started, and neither of us needed that," remembers Ted.

But the loneliness that was suffocating their relationship was heavier than the stack of bills on Ted's desk. The weight was too much to carry alone. Finally they sat down together and said, "This is ridiculous. We've got to stay in this together—sink or swim."

Now they know that the adversity of the last five years has made them a real team. Making a go of the business has been the right melding of their talents and gifts. It has taken everything they had to give. They have learned to respect and appreciate each other on a new level.

"I always knew that Ted was a natural leader," Anne says, "but that ability got overlooked during the time when we were just hanging on month-to-month." She has been able to stand back and watch his leadership abilities be refined under pressure. "I see Ted as the leader with a towel around his waist. He's not the slightest bit enamored with title and position. His natural strength has come back better than ever."

Ted credits Anne's innovation and ingenuity in design as the deciding human factor in keeping them from going over the edge of solvency. "People come in and take pictures of our design floor now. We're not just another floral business with boxes of fresh cut and dried flowers to pick from," he says. Her flair and style have shaped their niche in the marketplace.

Both of them have had the chance to watch each other survive some difficult situations. They know where they've failed. They also know they've both been able to "do some pretty amazing things through some pretty tough times."

"For one thing, we've gained a much broader understanding of the whole idea of roles in marriage," Ted explains. "Our lives are so integrated that the lines between who's-the-leader and who's-the-follower have kind of dissolved. We've just linked arms."

When they look back to where they were spiritually and relationally ten years ago, they see how far they've come. "Sometimes I think that if we've made it through this together, we can make it through almost anything. It's a good feeling," Anne says.

The intimacy they share now is what comes when a couple weathers stress and strain by choosing to pull together, and by capitalizing on the individual strengths that each one contributes to the whole.

GIVING EACH OTHER THE SPACE TO GROW

The third way to forge new connections actually contains a note of irony. Instead of enlarging the points on which their relationship overlaps, the couple begins to encourage each other's own individual bent.

The task that young married couples face is that of bonding together. After years of choosing their own preferences and schedules and idiosyncrasies, they learn to bend with the wishes of the other. If all goes as it should, two individuals are moving from independence to interdependence.

As a couple matures, however, the emphasis switches slightly. You begin, once again, to discover yourself and your mate as individuals. Now you experience not only the unity in your diversity, but the diversity in your unity.[5] You begin to see your mate as an individual again, one who is not like you or traveling exactly the same path as you.

When your own individuality is no longer easily threatened, you are better able to give your mate the space to grow. You stop trying so hard to script the other person into what you need him or her to be. It's like saying, "I don't have to make you be like me in order to feel good about myself." The irony is that you grow closer as you set each other free as individuals.

That is the process Grant and his wife found themselves going through. For years, their relationship revolved around his growing client load and the needs of their four children. Frequent moves that produced more acquaintances than friends added to their sense of isolation. His wife often felt that her focus had become so narrowed over years that she had little to contribute to their relationship. She felt lost in the shuffle. So Grant began to encourage her to discover her own interests and talents. He found that she needed confidence boosters, and now he knows that his opinion and support really matter to her. "I'm starting to see how much more multifaceted this woman is than I realized," he says, "and it's adding a new dimension to our relationship."

Thus, many couples deepen their relationship by encouraging each other's individuality or by facing outward adversity together and confronting their own inner fears. Yet a perfect relationship will never be ours this side of heaven. We are forever in process, moving toward a desire that will remain, in the deepest sense, unfulfilled. Even the best we now experience leaves us longing for more.

Perhaps what we learn after all these years is how much the world of relationships defies prescriptions and how-to formulas. In the final analysis, intimacy is more something we stumble upon rather than a state of being we can orchestrate—a peculiar kind of grace that comes long after we've searched the motivations of our own hearts and made some changes.

Private Tutoring in Relationships

In some ways, marriage is a microcosm of intimacy, a miniature laboratory for other close relationships. Martin Luther called marriage a school in which our character is built, a place where we learn how to release our grip on our oversized expectations and embrace another person for the individual he or she is. Those lessons spill over into other relationships as well.

Inside that laboratory, the very impasses that often serve to undermine intimacy in a relationship contain potential to make it new and rich and desirable. In his book *The Road Less Traveled*, M. Scott Peck writes about what a hopeful sign it is when a couple falls *out* of love. It gives them the chance "to initiate the work of real loving . . . it is when a couple falls out of love they may begin to really love."[6] We need to be the most determined at just the time when we are the most tempted to give up. Or as the women's columnist Judith Viorst quips, "One advantage of marriage is that when you fall out of love with him or he falls out of love with you, it keeps you together until you fall in love again."[7]

Just as individuals go through passages, so do marriages. We weather life together. Sometimes we forget that the relationship that began with vows and wedding cake edges forward, day by day, to a hill where a little green tent is pitched by a gravesite.

Stacy and I rarely make big occasions out of anniversaries, but two years ago we took an exception. We decided to cash in airline mileage on a special trip to England to celebrate our fifteen years together.

The grandparents came to take care of their grandchildren, and we gathered our travel brochures and camera and headed off for a week. Cotswald cottages, tea and scones at four o'clock—it would be the trip to beat all trips. And we did have a good time. Eight whole days without having to carpool the kids or get them to soccer practice can do a lot for any couple. But I had to admit that our trip hardly resembled the pictures in the advertisements.

For one thing, the prices were almost double those we remembered from ten years previous. Rain or unexpected crowds canceled a number of our plans. And those little Cotswald cottages had beds made for two of the seven dwarfs. We spent a few nights head to toe, and one, at least, with Stacy snoring peacefully on the floor beside me. Not exactly a second honeymoon.

Not until we were headed home did it strike me how fitting this trip to England had been to celebrated a marriage. Fifteen years before we set out on a lifetime journey together, every bit as starry-eyed as we had been just a week before. Instead of travel brochures, we had books and tapes and big ideas. We knew, or thought we knew, how to settle conflict, and what intimacy was supposed to look like. In other words, we had a lot of knowledge, but not much understanding.

We had not counted on spending half our marriage in school. Or selling a home for less than we bought it for. Or the changes in each other that required new, sometimes painful, adjustments. There is just so much that no one understands until he's been there himself.

Our trip—and our marriage—had been different than we expected. And in both cases, we had let individual events and ruffled feathers obscure the overall picture. Having children and renovating houses, straining to find each of our career niches—our relationship was more than the sum of those parts, just as our vacation couldn't be defined by the places we visited. In both cases, something far more significant was happening than the events themselves.

The point was, we had made the trip *together*. We were beginning to learn something about what it meant to keep company on cold nights.

Like many people in our generation, Stacy and I had hoped to find ecstasy in each other's arms. When we found something less than that, we did not know what to do with the disappointment. It took some time to see that we had actually stumbled onto something better than bliss. We discovered a love that is valuable precisely because it has been costly.

Not long after we returned from England, we were in McDonald's, which is still our children's favorite place to go. Our kids were busy dividing the french fries, piece by greasy piece lest one outdo the other, and Stacy was putting away his Big Mac. My attention was drawn to a retired couple seated right across the aisle. These days, older couples who seem to have weathered the years together well hold a peculiar fascination for me.

This couple appeared to have stopped to take a break from the road. Two cups of coffee were all their table held. With a burr haircut that stuck up like a mass of silver pins, the old farmer was in the middle of some tale. His wife stirred cream and sugar into both their cups, a habit so ingrained as to be second nature. She listened, not saying much, a smile playing about a face lined with age.

They had the kind of easy familiarity with each other where one sentence means a paragraph and the silences aren't heavy. I was struck by how thoroughly at home they seemed in each other's company. And I could not help but notice the way he reached for her hand as they walked back to their pickup truck.

I turned back to Stacy, who was in the final stages of arbitration over who had gotten the most of the fries. This was the man I wanted to grow old with—this fair-haired German with the mustache and the iron stomach. Thirty years from now, I wanted to stroll across a parking lot and have this guy reach for my hand.

Neither of us has lived up to all of the other's hopes. When it comes to whether or not I have fulfilled Stacy's fantasies, he has, no doubt, been forced to use some imagination. And every time I've tried to make him my knight in shining armor, we've both fallen off our horse. We've wasted enough time on small matters.

Our marriage is in a passage somewhere between the Beach Boys and Lawrence Welk—a little old for good vibrations and not quite ready for bubble music. Who knows how much time there is left? I only know that I want to dance while the music is still being played.

When I was a kid, I thought this was all just the beginning of the good times. I thought things would just get better from that point on.

Marie Callum, 35

9

Making It

When Less Starts to Seem Like Enough

Tucked away in a corner of our minds is harbored a picture of the good life. We collect images and store them there, like the little girl who flips through a dozen magazines until she gathers just the assortment of advertisements that strike her fancy. A dream home, a romantic vacation, a job that requires a sharp-looking suit, the right schools for the kids. We all know the basic building blocks for the American dream.

Most of us would hate to admit a correlation between that dream and our faith in and expectations of God. The "abundant life" found in Jesus did not necessarily mean an abundance of stuff. We knew it was not the same as the good life.

The problem was that the idealistic period of time that inflated our expectations of life coincided with the onset of the prosperity gospel. That was the idea that affluence and success were the marks of God's special blessing on His obedient children—a premise easily challenged by Scripture, however. The lives of Jeremiah and Paul and Jesus Christ hardly fit anyone's profile of prosperity. Unfortunately, the prosperity gospel fit well with many current, but temporary, financial trends of the time—the oil boom of the '70s and the inflated stock market of the '80s. Although we noted the theological error in it, the prosperity gospel wreaked havoc on our subconscious. Maybe God's blessing could indeed be measured in dollars and cents. Perhaps God does want me to be rich. Maybe I really am what I own.

The last twenty-five years have contained numerous financial cycles, periods of expansions and prosperity followed closely by recession and cutbacks. Many of us have felt whiplashed by the roller coaster nature of those cycles, confused as to exactly what it means to experience the goodness of God in our lives.

Whether we have connected our material dreams with our faith or not, the good life is getting harder and harder to get. While our Depression-era parents considered a college education or owning your own car to be a privilege—the icing on their cake—we viewed those things as part of the cake. The good life was that plus a whole lot more. "Did we really set out to have it all?" I asked a friend once. "Not exactly," she replied. "I just want a little bit of all of it."

Our generation spawned Donald Trump. He is one of us. Like Donald, many of us experienced the contraction of our dreams rather than the continued expansion we hoped for. The statistics on our generation, taken as a whole, are somewhat sobering. Though 5 to 10 percent of us actually live the lives depicted on slick magazine covers, the vast majority of us are not projected to fare nearly as well as our parents have. We have not grown richer as we have grown older, the way wine improves with age. The average income of a person aged twenty-five to thirty-four has been declining for ten years straight. There are forty thousand Ph.D.s in our generation who cannot get jobs in their field. Fewer jobs, fewer promotions, lower relative wages—the litany goes on and on. Maybe the Rolling Stones were right—you can't always get what you want.

Many of us are straddled between more options and fewer means. "I've got the education and the ability to do a variety of jobs," explains a man in his early thirties, who has spent the last several years trying to find his niche in sales. "I'm not like my father. I don't have to spend my life in one job working in a bank like he did."

Instead, there are a host of different arenas in which he could maximize his talents. But he hadn't counted on how quickly those options could dry up in a downturned economy. "Trying to match up available jobs with my skills and my mortgage payment hasn't been easy," he says. He can see what he wants. It's within his reach, but always a little beyond his grasp.

Scenarios like his, repeated dozens of times, explain why fully one-third of our generation is disappointed in what they have achieved thus far in life.[1] There is a persistent feeling that "I ought to be further along than I am." How much further? Research shows that most of us live by the "25 percent rule."[2] We need 25 percent more money or status or achievement to feel successful. And success, for a generation for whom the "icing" has become the "cake," is a constantly moving target.

We get caught between the life we had and the life we would like to provide for our children. One woman, whose father and husband are both small town dentists, mirrored well that squeeze. "Our children look at their grandfather in his sports car coming home from some big trip and they want to know why we're still driving a station wagon," she says. She tries to explain that their father is as good a dentist as their grandfather but that times are just different.

"When I was growing up," she remembers, "my parents set aside $700 a year, and we toured a different region of the country every summer. Now we could hardly take our kids to an average motel at the beach for a week on that amount."

For the most part she was not too bothered by the discrepancy in her husband's income and her father's— until she reached her late thirties. "Before then I just assumed it was all up ahead, around the next corner," she says. "Lately, I've started to realize that we may never get to the place, like my parents, where we can just coast."

But no matter what we have or have not achieved thus far in life, many of us arrive in our thirties with a curious sense of deflation. After graduate school, after we've had a few children, after we've redecorated the house, then what? What's next? we ask. Surely there is more.

"I was content to move from place to place while my husband finished medical school and his residency," confides a wife who has packed and unpacked too many boxes in her day. After years of the gypsy life, they settled down in a small town in Virginia's Shenandoah Valley. Her husband put his diplomas on the wall and a brass nameplate on the door. They bought a new home in a nice neighborhood and put the children in school. "Then," she says, "it was like we turned to each other and said, 'This is it?'" That was it.

Sooner or later we lose faith in the idea that one more achievement or one more degree will finally put us "over the top." We will never again feel like the junior high kid with gum stuck in his braces. "I was finally able to open up my own law firm in the town where I grew up in," says a man who paid his dues working for someone else for ten years. The thrill didn't last long, though. "When all is said and done," he explains, "I really own a shop on main street where I sell law advice. It's not all that special. I'm not too different from a kid with his lemonade stand."

No matter how much or how little we have partaken of the dream, we still have an insistent urge to experience the parts that are missing. If we have excelled in accomplishments, we may be searching for relationships. And if friends and family abound, we are looking for ways to test our abilities to achieve. What we don't have tends to look far more attractive than what we have.

Cheryl Merser, in her book about growing up and growing older in this generation, talks about how she realized that she had a job in a New York City publishing house that others envied. The book she had just written adorned her coffee table. But the farther she got into her thirties, the more lonely she became. "So what if I had written a book?" she says. "Now I looked at my book, sitting on my coffee table, in disgust. You can't kiss a book good morning, or make love to it at night, tuck it in and read it a story, or carry its picture around in your wallet. You can't even wash clothes in it. What good is a book?"[3]

So it is that a many of us arrive in our late thirties and early forties with our images of the good life either evaporating or taking on an entirely new shape. We scale down our expectations, or redefine them, and try to disconnect our ideas about the American Dream from the promises of God.

More Pressure, Harder Choices

So what do you do when you wake up one day and realize that the big chunk of your life is behind you and you still haven't arrived? Your life doesn't measure up to the mural you had painted in that tiny corner of your mind.

That's not an easy idea to face when you can hear the relentless ticking of your own internal clock. After all, whatever it is that you're going to do or be or achieve or experience, you had better get after it. Time is running out. It's too late to be a trapeze artist or a belly dancer or a nun. Some possibilities have already been eliminated. One life is all you get, one trip around the game board, and you aren't allowed to go past "Go" again and collect another $200.

That creates pressure. More pressure to achieve and acquire, to hang on to a job you dislike for the security it represents, to buy when you should rent, to build when it would be wiser to remodel. The modern workplace and lifestyle exact a high emotional toll, as psychologist Douglas LaBier found when he studied the lives of 230 people between the ages of twenty-five and forty-seven.[4] Our age group is overrun with anxiety, burnout, and the stress of straining to reach the elusive target of "making it," whatever that means.

"I wish I could remember how to relax," says a man nearing forty who wonders if he'll ever get out of the middle management pool. He admits that he frequently flips to the radio station that plays "Venus in Blue Jeans" and other classic pieces of serious musicians. "It takes me back to an era in my life when I could spend days with my feet in the sand, a beer in my hand, listening to the waves pound the beach like there was no tomorrow," he says. Now he can hardly find his way to the beach, and when he does he's got a briefcase of work under one arm and his children's rafts under the other. By the time he unwinds it's time to head for home.

This is the point, in the middle of life, where we cross the invisible line that causes our focus to shift from how many years we have lived to how many years we have left. Life takes on that "last chance" feeling. If you ever hope to get that degree or raise the venture capital for your own business or uproot to a totally new location, there is no better time than now. Things that were just possibilities before now appear urgent as you weigh the risks versus the benefits perceived. The question becomes, How much present security are you willing to give up in order to reach out for something different?

"Suppose I never do leave teaching—which seems like a rut that I've worn too smooth—and go back to school in computer programming? Can I make it another twenty-five years in this field, and if I do, will I become a dehydrated fruit in the process? Can our budget stretch far enough to let me try something new?" A hundred questions like these clamor for answers because the answers affect not just our own life but the lives of everyone close to us.

As our responsibilities increase and our physical stamina wanes, we face hard choices. Opportunities we have worked years for may unfold at the same time that other demands on our life and challenges with our children reach a high water mark. We shift into overdrive and rev up the old adrenalin once again.

But now your body refuses to cooperate. If you burn the candle at both ends for too long at this point in life, you may find there's no wick left to catch fire. "No matter how hard I try," complains one nurse with three children, "I can't push any harder than I'm already pushing. There's nothing left to push with."

Somewhere between the ages of thirty-five and forty-five, our responsibilities collide headlong with our capacity to perform. We are hamstrung between the demands on our life and our capacity to meet those demands. The responsibilities have increased but our stamina has not. When that happens, the real tests of character and values come to the fore. "What will I have to jettison?" we ask. "What do I want to keep, and what do I need to let go of?"

Most of us don't see those choices coming before they are upon us, nor do we anticipate the pressure that accompanies them. That's what Grant realized when he established his psychiatric practice outside a large, metropolitan city. He had expected to bury himself in the task of sorting out the problems of hurting people who came for help. But fifteen years ago, when he chose psychiatry as his specialty, he had not foreseen the day when someone who could integrate Christianity and psychology would be in such demand.

Now his weekly mail includes invitations to speak and to give seminars on a variety of topics that genuinely interest him. He is nearing a place in his own development where he believes he has something to say. He has always wanted to publish, and that no longer looks like a pipe dream.

His only problem is that his opportunities are coinciding with a time when his four children are quickly growing up. They have their own dreams, dreams that need a father's encouragement. Sometimes he feels pulled apart at the seams. "I can't afford to get where I want to go at my kids' expense," he says. "I see too much of that in my office every day." He knows that if you have to steal from your kids in order to make it, in the long run you may lose on both counts.

But he still feels caught in a vise, afraid that if he passes up these opportunities now, he may not have another chance. He admits that he is the one who usually pays the price, through lack of sleep and days off, for trying to keep too much going at once. He realizes that he is living without a margin and that his days of being able to do so are numbered.

Grant is facing the fact that as the demands on him have increased, he has a limited reservoir of energy to meet them. Like him, many of us experience similar pressure in this stage in life to establish some clear goals that help us let go of or postpone lesser priorities. The good life is a lesser life if it forces us to run twice as fast just to keep up.

How to Know When You've Made It

If anyone had ever asked me what was the predominant image on that mural of the good life in my mind, I would have said a house. Not just any house, though—a turn-of-the-century home decorated with a few antiques and wood floors and a staircase. I wasn't thinking big; a cozy place with gables and high ceilings would do fine. Over the years, with each of our moves, that picture became clearer in my mind.

Yet with every move, we seemed to acquire a new skill in our ability to chose a housing market higher than the one we were leaving. Like so many Americans and so many people our age, our tastes always exceeded our means.

Moving back east to North Carolina was the hardest move of all. Never had I seen such a wealth of old houses to choose from. Why, if I kept redefining my concept of old, we could buy a house that predated World War I, or the Civil War, or for that matter, the original revolt from England. Just how old a house did I want, anyway?

Every day I looked at houses, I felt as though I was on a great treasure hunt. I lay awake at night plotting my strategy to transform the wonderful old monstrosity I had seen that day into a restored masterpiece fit for the cover of *Southern Living.*

Like a child in a candy store, though, I kept forgetting to count the change in my purse. My husband and the loan officer at the bank had to jog my memory. We could not afford a turn-of-the-century home. Again. It was that simple. After five moves and two other attempts, we were going to have to buy a house in *this* century, and probably the most recent half at that. By the time we could afford the kind of house with gables and a staircase, I might well be wallpapering the foyer from my electric wheelchair.

An old house, restored to the luster of a warmer era, had always represented for me a place of safety and security. That was "making it" in my mind—the invitation to kick off my shoes, sit back, and rest a spell.

Everyone, I'm convinced, has a similar picture, some dream that lures them forward and promises relief from the daily grind. Advertising and marketing gurus know best how to tap into those images, and then add a little paint to our brush. They help us turn a desire into a full-fledged need.

It is possible, however, in this world of difficult choices and doused hopes, for us to paint over parts of the good-life mural. There are unexpected places where less starts to seem like more.

WHEN WE FIND A DIFFERENT MEASURING STICK

Often beneath the rubble of a disappointed dream, lies a treasure or two that we could never have seen while we were so bent on realizing our hope. One of those concerns the inner criteria by which we measure success. Our ideals change as our hopes are transformed.

When Ted was at the height of his financial crisis, for instance, and was convinced that his business might go under, he kept hoping that God would come to his rescue on a grand scale. But the "miracle" never came. Instead, he hung on for months, with finances the ever-present issue and failure looming large before him.

Only as time afforded him perspective could he begin to see that the business was making forward progress, inch by inch. Answers to his prayer were coming in dribbles, not downpours—in such small increments, in fact, that Ted could not rest on the laurels of being the "young, successful entrepreneur" he had once hoped to become.

When he was finally allowed some breathing room and finances were no longer a constant matter of survival, he found that a curious thing had taken place. He had developed a new criteria for what success looked and felt like. He was holding a different yardstick.

"I noticed, for the first time, that I had grown to feel immense pleasure in the work we were doing. In a world where Madonna gets rave reviews, we were offering a product of real quality, and I began to let myself enjoy that," he says. "I've come to think that there is a peculiar pleasure God gives a person when he's in his element, his niche—a kind of joy in the work itself."

He also began to reap the benefits among his employees from all the months of having to pull together. In the process of learning how to resolve conflict, they had become a team. The pleasure in those relationships is, again, something Ted had never before considered in his concept of success. Should the business climate improve, Ted believes he has the foundation necessary to take advantage of it. He admits that had he been able to reach his earlier business goals and spin off new floral franchises, he would probably never have slowed down long enough to savor any of it.

In *Downshifting,* business writer Amy Saltzman chronicles the lives of people in our generation who have made conscious choices to redefine the way they measure success. The plateauer, the back-tracker, the career-shifter, the self-employer, and the urban escapee represent five kinds of people who decided to leave the fast lane in favor of a saner, more satisfying lifestyle. Saltzman uses their examples to challenge us to "reinvent" our notions of success and to adopt new "success imagery" that allows us to slow down and enjoy more of life.

Ted is enjoying a good life—it's just not the one he had expected. His story is an example of what often happens when reality does not measure up to our expectations. As we let go of the false images in our minds, we develop a new, truer definition of success.

WHEN WE DISCOVER WHAT WE REALLY WANT

Another area where less can begin to seem like more is on the level of our deepest desires.

Sometimes our dreams, especially the ones built on advertising pictures of the good life, serve only to camouflage our true desires. I may think, for instance, that I want a Victorian gingerbread house with lace doilies and the smell of cinnamon throughout. That's what I have been conditioned to think I want, anyway. But in reality, if I probe a little deeper, I am really after the warmth and intimacy of the relationships that I perceive exist in such a picture. If I ask myself what I *really* want, I uncover intangibles that can't be acquired like items on a shopping list.

The problem is that most of us are so driven in our pursuit of that enticing dream that we don't stop long enough to identify what it really is. Our energy is consumed by the effort to realize our dreams, to finally come to the elusive point where we feel like we've arrived. Our question is, How can I get there—wherever *there* is? And we ask it so persistently that we never get to the questions that follow. We don't get the chance to move from, "How can I get there?" to, "Where am I trying to get?" and, finally, "What if I did?"

So we fall prey to all sorts of advertising come-ons. I think of one, for example, a personal invitation in the mail that many people our age receive. It tries hard to be impressive, and, if by chance we don't answer it the first time, we will receive another opportunity soon. It is from American Express, who would like to place a plastic card in our hand that will open the doors to all the things we ever wanted.

They know the right words to say. They are sending you this special invitation because "you are a person who will appreciate this most honored and prestigious financial instrument . . . the sense of self-esteem, the recognition, and the security that come from carrying the world's most respected card." Security, prestige, recognition. Here, supposedly, is your ticket.

I happened to read these words over my husband's shoulder on the day they landed in our mailbox, and together we smiled. "It's nice to be pursued, if only for our money," he mused.

The question occurred to me, "What would you want if you had the cars and trips and the long business lunches this card seems to promise?" But what I said was, "What would you want then?" I watched him chew on that for a while, waiting for his response, not even sure what my own would be.

His answer caught me off guard. I expected to hear him say something outlandish, like a kid with three wishes and a genie in his bottle. He said that after he had gotten the dreams that card symbolized, he'd probably pack up and take the kids camping.

"Camping?" I said. "You would take the kids camping?"

Yes, he assured me. But that wasn't all. "I guess I'd be looking for some good friends, for a sense of impact on my world, maybe a deeper connection with the Lord." And for good measure, an expanded schedule of racquetball—something as uncomplicated as a good chance to sweat.

That was what he would really want?

When he finished, we both stopped. Like two minds in syncopated rhythm, it hit us. What we really wanted—genuine relationships, a sense of impact, time to enjoy life—did not require a plastic card. Maybe we had gotten so attached to our dreams that we forgot the point. Perhaps we were only beginning to uncover our true desires. In other words, what we really wanted was more accessible than we thought. In fact, *it was a lot of what we already had.*

Our generation and those coming after us are often called "the disenfranchised generation." The good life we were raised to think we would inherit is slipping through our fingers. The problem is not that we want too much.

Our desires are not too strong; they are just uninformed. It seems to take almost half a lifetime and the disappointment of some of our dreams to come to terms with what we really want out of life.

Perhaps our generation, whether by choice or default, will be the first to redesign our ideas about what exactly constitutes the good life. Maybe we will be the ones to admit that even a beach in Tahiti is pretty barren without the peace of mind and depth of relationships to fill out the scene. And that if you had to choose, at least you would know what choice to make, because you know what it is you really want.

Sometimes I find myself sitting on our front porch out under the shade of tall pine trees. The red brick of our ranch home frames a blue Carolina sky and seems to beg for geraniums and impatiens to line its borders.

I stare at gutters, not gables, and the only staircase is the one that leads to the front door. Inside there are offices in strange places, a kitchen being remodeled, and three bedrooms in need of fresh paint. A few antiques and wood floors are scattered throughout, but basically the house represents another compromise. It is not my dream home; its bricks were laid too recently. It dates back to the wrong war—the one in Vietnam.

My own ideas about the good life are changing slowly. Although this house fails to live up to the mural in my mind and it's not my picture of the good life, who knows? If we stay here another ten years we will finally own a turn-of-the-century home.

The turn of the next century.

You've got to experience the bottom of life falling out a couple of times and God somehow being there in the midst of it. All of that happens in your thirties, and that's where a person really encounters God.

Roger Randall, 41

10

An Honest Faith

Moving Beyond Simple Answers

Disappointments come in all kinds of shapes and sizes, weights and measures. Some merely glance off you sideways, like tiny beads of sleet on the arm of a stadium jacket. You can feel the ping, but it's not bad enough to run for cover. But other disappointments penetrate. They cut to the core like a knife, leaving you with the feeling that you have been split apart and left in sections.

Letting go of old dreams is, for anyone, an inevitable part of maturing. No one gets through life with all his or her dreams intact. But when a particular hope is fueled and carried forward on faith—when it's hard to tell where the dream stops and your faith begins—that kind of disappointment is no ordinary loss. It is the deepest disappointment of all, and it strikes a double blow because it threatens our understanding of God.

Susan's story is a good example of a broken dream that challenges the foundations of a person's faith and ability to trust God. When she met and married Jim, she thought she was pursuing a direction that had all the marks of God's blessing. Their relationship was built on common beliefs and shared values, undergirded by the sense that God had something special planned for them as a couple. They had a solid spiritual foundation from which to build a lifetime together.

Yet within the first few years of marriage, Susan became more and more aware that something was chipping away at that foundation. Jim's struggles with his father, his inner restlessness and frustration only seemed to grow, as though it were fed from a spring whose source neither of them could locate.

During their last six months together, Jim's personality began to show signs of drastic change. He started devising elaborate means to be everywhere but home. He had another life—business, nightclubs, and who knew what else—and it became more obvious that Susan was not invited to be a part. More and more, they were living in two separate worlds, and the wall between them was not one Susan could scale alone.

When Susan was six months pregnant with their second child, Jim told her that he would stay long enough for the baby to be born. But then he wanted a place of his own.

Kelsey, their second little girl, arrived on schedule, an easy baby with bright eyes and full of life. There were moments in the hospital when Susan was sure she saw a hint of tenderness in Jim's face when he held her. She continued to pray, more hopefully now, that God would intervene in their lives through this tiny infant.

Jim brought everyone home, posed for a few pictures, and played the part of a dutiful daddy—for a few weeks, anyway. But his restlessness, that subterranean anger, returned, and this time, the normal family forces that would keep him home only seemed to repel him all the more for their intensity. He was living on the edge.

Jim left one day when Susan had taken both girls to the doctor. She found the note on the kitchen table and his closet emptied. Her first reaction was that for once Jim had been totally true to his word. He had stayed long enough for Kelsey to be born.

A protective numbness set in, which prevented Susan from feeling the full effect of what was happening to her. For a while, she let herself be lost in the constant demands of a toddler and a nursing baby. But her money was running out, and Jim was filing for divorce. When her parents offered to drive down from Oregon and help her move back there, she reluctantly agreed. She didn't know what else to do.

The full weight of reality fell upon her as she was turning into the driveway of the home she had grown up in. She had trouble finding the car door handle for the tears that were streaming down her face. This was not the way you were supposed to come home—with two small children in the back seat and your father pulling a U-Haul with the contents of your home behind you. It was like waking up to a bad dream.

Susan slowly began to establish a new life. She got a job in public relations for a pharmaceutical firm, and her mother helped out with the girls. In haphazard form, Susan managed to put back a few of the pieces of her life. But underneath the edges of that cut-and-paste job, she was raw on the inside. She felt alone and abandoned by her husband—and on a more profound level, by God. Why had He seemed present in their courtship and so absent during the last two years of their marriage? How had He let this happen?

Those were the kinds of questions brewing inside Susan, but she tried to ignore them. She stayed clear of the Christian community, afraid that her disillusionment would show. Besides, the sound of church music had a disturbing tendency to make her cry. She found herself unable to turn to God. Just a look in His direction stirred memories of her relationship with Jim—warm memories of old times when they prayed together, of how right their relationship had felt, of all the spiritual hopes they had shared. Her faith, her ability to trust God, was tied up in those dreams, and she had no idea how to unravel such a tangled knot.

She tried not to think too hard, but sometimes her dreams betrayed her, as her mind continued to search for resolution while she slept. One dream, in particular, stayed with her during all the months that her divorce dragged on. In her dream, she saw a woman dressed in a white robe go past her bedroom door. Her face was radiant, like the spirit of God, and many people were following her. Then in a few minutes, Susan saw the same woman come by her door again. This time she hobbled by with the help of a cane, her face drawn and distorted with horrible bitterness and hate.

At that point Susan bolted awake and almost by reflex found herself praying. "Oh, God," she said, "don't let me become that bitter old woman."

Susan's dream of a warm, intimate marriage ended, as many do, in divorce. And when marriage ends, there is heartache and grief. But because the steps that led her toward her dream were steps of *faith,* filled with the patchwork of answered prayer and special circumstances, Susan was left with troubling doubts and questions. A marriage made in heaven is not supposed to end in a divorce court.

For those who know what it is to wed hope to faith, we empathize with the inner struggle that resonates beneath the pain of such a loss. Trusting God was the anchor to which many in our generation tied their dreams. In the throes of disappointment, we are left with one question—if we let go of our dream, or if it is wrested from us, then will we lose, along with it, our ability to trust God in any true measure? As one woman voiced after years of infertility and miscarriages ended in a hysterectomy: "I would not have dared to hope so hard or so long except that I thought God was in it. When I realized that He wasn't, I felt as though I had been dancing with a lion." She struggled not only with the loss of a dream, but with how that loss had undermined her faith as well.

When hope that was once closely tied to faith is dashed—a fairly common dilemma in our generation—a person is left with unsettling emotions and inner turmoil.

Sometimes people talk of losing their spiritual bearings, as though they had been led down a particular road that suddenly became a blind alley. Fog settles in, and so much of what once seemed clear and simple no longer is. This is the natural point where one would perhaps turn to God—but His whereabouts have never seemed less certain. It appears as though He has defeated His own purposes and become, if not the author of our disappointment, at least an accomplice.

When the Box Crumbles

Whereas an experience of that nature can be trying, it nevertheless represents a critical juncture in the development of a person's faith. We are presented with the opportunity to let go of a faith that is often, in reality, not faith at all. It is akin to a *manageable belief system*, where faithfulness or obedience on our part seems to obligate God to fulfill our desires. Faith, as a manageable belief system, is a faith that insists. What we are asked to embrace at this juncture in life is an *open-ended trust*, where we let go of our efforts to control the outcome of following God.

In some ways I am describing a kind of reconversion—a new turning, a deep inner response to a Person so "wholly other" that He can't be exhausted by our concepts, our words, our imaginations, or our expectations. A Person who encourages and challenges, supports and frustrates, serves and demands. Someone different from what we had in mind, but the one we needed all along.

In many ways, this is an inevitable and much-needed turn in our spiritual journey because we all begin with constricted, one-dimensional ideas about what God is like. I think of a wise old seminary processor I once knew who began his class each fall, a class usually filled with bright, idealistic young men and women, by asking one simple question.

He walked into class on the first day, took a seat on the corner of his desk with his legs swinging back and forth, and said, "Students, I have one question for you. What is God like?"

His students get their pens and notebooks in position, ready to hear the answer from the professor. But he doesn't say a word. He sits waiting for their response. In desperation, one student after another tries to fill the awkward pauses. God is love, God is justice, God is this, God is that. The professor just sits there looking out the window, totally unimpressed. Finally, after the class has exhausted everything they ever knew or heard or conceived about God, the professor begins to speak.

"Men and women, let me tell you something," he says. "God is not like *anything*. And the tragedy is that you are going to build your little theological boxes around what you think God is like, and someday when you really need Him, you're going to race to your box and open the lid and *He won't be in there.*"

By that point, his class is speechless, shaking their heads in disbelief and wondering what he means. It usually takes another twenty years of maturity and the experience of having the bottom fall out a time or two before they begin to understand the wisdom in his words.

Perhaps most of us start out just like those young seminary students, wanting something predictable and sure and concrete. Human nature begs to construct a picture of what we think God is like, a kind of spiritual box we can fit Him into. We want a fix on God. The how-to formulas are actually comforting—tangible evidence that things will work out the way we want them to.

The kind of disappointment or letdown that jars our faith, though, also causes the walls of that box to dissolve. The spiritual territory here is uncharted and sometimes frightening. Perhaps you took a wrong turn to arrive at such a place. You don't know what else lurks in the darkness. As one friend said, "Suddenly, I realized that if the thing I feared had happened, then almost anything else was possible, too. I no longer felt safe."

Can't I just return to the days when faith seemed sure

and simple? Can't I go back to where I was? Those are natural questions to ask. We long for a Bible study or spiritual retreat or earnest effort or *something* that promises that old certainty. We long for faith to lose its tentative feel—to cease to feel like faith.

There is no going back, though. Our manageable belief system no longer works so well. The walls of the box begin to crumble. God often seems strangely absent, as though He has left us on our own to sort things out. Yet, in reality, what we are experiencing is this pain and confusion of letting go, not of God, but of the safe, secure confines we built to house our concept of Him. God is not a concept to be mastered, a set of prescriptions we can control. He shows Himself to be much different than we thought—more loving, more exacting, more faithful.

We are being readied to take our first steps toward the freedom of relaxing in the embrace of one who is both big enough and strong enough to contain our doubts, to comfort our disappointments, and to confront our prodigal hearts.

However, in the midst of this kind of faith transition, more than our concept of God is challenged. We may also begin to gain deeper insight into our own motivation. Disappointed hopes often reveal the stuff we're made of—both good and bad. We see how weak our own loyalties can be, how riddled with self-seeking our faith was all along.

When Ted was at his lowest point financially, only a few steps from having to declare bankruptcy, he had an encounter with a good friend that jarred him in a personal and spiritual sense. He was busy adding up figures and reviewing delinquent accounts one day, when he looked up from his desk long enough to see a new Mercedes being parked right outside his window. Out stepped his friend, Dave, with a grin on his face like a Cheshire cat.

He burst through the door of Ted's office, barely able to contain himself. "You won't believe this," he said. Dave went on to tell him that he had just put together a deal for a strip shopping mall that no one thought had a ghost of a chance. Now he was beaming with good fortune. The commission would carry him through the next several years quite well.

Ted did his best to share in Dave's excitement, but inside he felt like a big fake. The whole conversation couldn't end fast enough for him. It took about a half hour for Dave to wind down, and when Ted finally closed the door behind him, he let out a great sigh of relief. Then he turned back to his desk and kicked the metal trash can against the wall as hard as he could. Why did everyone seem to have the magic formula but him? Where was God?

Ted felt like he was being eaten alive with envy. He could not begin to be genuinely happy for his friend because his own concerns got in the way. It was one of his worst moments. As he realized that, an image of Jesus suddenly came to his mind and he was stunned by the contrast. In Christ's worst moments, what had He been like? He had cared about the people around Him. Love controlled Him.

The stark contrast between Ted's response and the one he saw in Jesus moved him to a profound sense of worship and awe. One small phrase spoken by the father of the disgruntled prodigal son came to mind. "I have always loved you and all that I have is yours," the father had said.[1] Ted realized that God was working differently in his life than in his friend's but no less graciously.

So it is that in facing disappointment, much shifts inside us, much changes about the way we view our faith and ourselves.

An Honest Heart

What is necessary in order to build the kind of open-ended trust that marks genuine spiritual growth? Perhaps, to begin with, that transition requires an honest heart, a response more difficult than it sounds. Facing disappointment with God often means sorting through a tangled knot of emotions—anger, grief, rebellion, bewilderment. Such messy scenes may be permissible with a friend or spouse or even one of our children. But God? For Him, we tend to make ourselves more presentable, to stay dressed in our Sunday best. It's easier to paste a smile on our face and pretend. To be honest with God at the level of disappointment seems a gutsy proposition.

When the miscarriage of a dream seems hopelessly intertwined with your faith, when in some crazy way it was *God* who didn't live up to your expectations, the most natural inclination is simply to turn away from Him. That kind of backward motion can be accomplished in a variety of ways, both subtle and blatant. Some people escape into an affair, or pursue a sport or graduate school or a new business idea with renewed vigor. But more often, we choose more subtle means of giving up, much like letting the air leak slowly out of your tires until you are left stranded. The most effective means of turning away, however, is never to admit that you were even disappointed.

After Susan returned home with two small children in tow, she kept herself distracted with the business of starting life over. There was plenty to keep her occupied. She noticed, from time to time, how rarely she prayed, and that when she did, it was superficial. Her Bible was tucked away in a bedroom drawer she had not opened for months. None of this was by design exactly. It just happened that way.

Sudden outbursts of frustration with her kids seemed to come from nowhere, and they frightened her. She had a strong urge to slam the door on her boss every time she walked out of his office. Cynical thoughts played around the edge of her mind, but for the most part, she managed to keep them to herself.

It was a friend's offhand remark that got her attention. Susan had just spent an hour complaining to her about tight finances. As her friend reached for the restaurant bill, she remarked, "You sound like a pretty angry woman."

Susan was taken aback. Could it be that she was hiding anger behind her cool front? Maybe she was angry—and hurt and disappointed as well.

That Jim was the focal point of that anger and pain was obvious. His face was the clearest one in her mind. She was down on herself, too. What was hardest for Susan to face was her anger with God. She felt as though He had betrayed her, even though she knew her decision to marry Jim had been her own choice.

There is at least one example in the Bible of someone whose spiritual struggle centered around feelings of betrayal. Jeremiah, who was drafted by God into a post as a prophet in Judah, knew that the task of being God's spokesman to a rebellious nation was no dream job. He knew he would encounter the wrath of kings and the deaf ear of his countrymen. But when a fellow priest named Pashhur had Jeremiah beaten and put into stocks, Jeremiah sank to an all-time low. He did not seem to be prepared for opposition from another "servant of God."

At that point, Jeremiah's story stops, and we are given audience to a profoundly personal prayer, revealing a man struggling with the unexpected circumstances God had allowed in his life. "O Lord," Jeremiah says, "Thou hast deceived me and I was deceived; Thou has overcome me and prevailed."[2] Jeremiah began to pray about his confusion. He admitted the worst of it. "I feel betrayed, let down, angry, and overcome," he said. On one level, he felt deceived by God, and on another he knew he had deceived himself. He made no attempt to sort it all out—he simply brought the whole tangled mess to the Lord. He counted on the strength of one who could bear the weight of such honesty.

When Susan got the courage to bring an honest heart to God and allowed herself to admit the anger and disappointment she felt, she was surprised. "It was as though God had been waiting all that time for me to invite Him into the middle of my situation," she says. "It was like He stepped out from behind a curtain. After months and months of feeling almost no connection with Him at all, I was bowled over by the immediacy of His presence."

Slowly, mysteriously, the ability to forgive Jim, other Christians, even God, began to take shape. "I've come to think," Susan says now, "that forgiveness in places where there's been a lot of hurt is really something supernatural, a gift as well as a choice."

Gathering the courage to be honest, to stop running and hiding and pretending brings tremendous freedom. We come empty handed to the Lord, carrying nothing but an open heart, and God takes that honesty and transforms it into a kind of saving grace.

Disappointment: An Unlikely Route to Faith

Learning to be honest with God was the first step for Susan, a new chapter in the slow process of rebuilding her life. She began to realize that for years she possessed a "lazy man's faith," where she simply accepted whatever someone told her. She had never taken it out and examined it for herself.

When she began to do that, for a while everything was up for question. "I started over from scratch," she says. "The most I could say at some points was that there is a God and He sent Jesus to die for my sins. Slowly, I've added more back, and what I have now is mine, really mine."

Susan speaks with the quiet confidence of someone who has experienced a deep spiritual renewal, a reconversion. What she believes and the way she feels are an integrated whole. She has the freedom to question. "I wouldn't wish this kind of pain on anyone," she says, "but in many ways the best thing that ever happened to me was that it all fell apart."

Who would guess that faith itself would be one of those things you have to lose in order to find it, that it's possible to be less sure of the answers and more certain of God, or that when you finally let go of the determination to make God conform in safe, predictable ways, you receive something better in its place?

I am convinced that real faith is alien to human nature. It's not part of the air I breathe. What for years I passed off as faith was little more than an effort to take what I understood about God and shape that knowledge into something I could get my hands around. Like the constitution of the United States, faith was a set of propositions to be analyzed, explained, and defended with your blood.

I suspect that much of what I formerly called faith is little better than having invited God into the parlor of my life while I checked His references. I was not sure that I could risk giving Him the full run of the place. Sometimes I have felt frustrated with His apparent absence, wondering why He seldom seemed present in a more immediate way. And at other times I have wanted Him to go away and leave me be, like a UPS delivery man who kept bringing packages to my door that I did not order.

What I see in Susan's life, though, and what I sense God is moving me toward, is something qualitatively different. It is a faith that looks more like an open hand than a clenched fist—a faith that is wide and free and at ease with uncertainty.

This kind of open-ended trust always seems to come unexpectedly. It comes only after you've been disillusioned with what seemed like faith, only after some stinging disappointment causes your box to collapse. The utter paradox is that this kind of trust begins in those unlikely moments when there is no experiential reason to believe. Only then is there room for real faith to take root. It is born in the fearlessness that comes when you've already lost a good portion of what you were so afraid of losing in the first place. It sprouts at a point of contradiction.

There are three basic options in our response to life and faith, explains Gerald May in his book *Addiction and Grace*. The first is that we ignore God's call on our lives and turn our desires and energies elsewhere. That is simple enough. Second, we can fashion a spiritual system that will enable us to feel a measure of power and control rather than dependence. In an absurd way, we use what we know about God to try to keep Him contained. Or we may finally choose what May calls the contemplative option, which he says signals the beginning of "an intentional spiritual life." The contemplative option is a willingness

"to face life in a truly undefended and open-eyed way.-
. . . [It] is a simple courageous attempt to bear as much as
one can of reality just as it is."³ Not pretending, not running away, but facing life head-on.

The movement toward genuine faith is marked by
choosing to trust God even when we know that the outcome
may be far different than we had ever imagined. We let go of
our preconceived notions of how things ought to be. If life
is a river, we jump right out into the middle of the stream
and let it take us where it will. Our trust is open-ended.

That kind of faith is new to me. I hardly know how to
make my way around in it yet. Spiritual prescriptions and
techniques on how to live the Christian life—I have a
whole repertoire of those. But I am just now moving beyond the simple answers into a place where I can enjoy a
relationship with a Person, sometimes elliptical, full of
ebb and flow, desert and garden. I am learning to let the
dissonance feed my newfound trust.

Maybe we who speak of "receiving Christ" do ourselves an injustice by connecting the phrase purely with
the act of becoming a Christian. In actuality, we receive
Him not once, but many, many times throughout our lives.
That is why disappointment with God can be such an effective catalyst for faith, a ripening of trust that is born on
His terms. Sometimes it is as fresh as conversion. When
that begins to happen, we once again encounter the hidden wealth in a disappointed dream.

Growing up spiritually means progressing through a
series of "ifs." We begin by wondering "what if": What if
this happens or that happens? Can I make it? Can I find a
way to keep my fears from taking over? Or we dabble in a
lot of "if onlys": If only I had a better job or house or marriage, my life would be set. I would be happy.

But real faith means moving to another kind of "if"
entirely. Even if. Even if my marriage fails or the roof over
my head falls—no matter what—you can count me in. I'm
here for the long haul because I realize there is no one
else to turn to, and nowhere else I'd rather be.

Under those coats and ties, my generation is as activistic and idealistic as it ever was. They're just waiting to rediscover the sense of mission they once had.

Jack Simms, 39

11
Saving the World
What Happened When We Didn't

On a recent summer trip overseas with my husband, I happened on an unusual opportunity. I was invited to join fifteen others on an old fishing boat leaving for a snorkeling expedition off the coast of Malaysia in the South China Sea. They had room for one more passenger. I packed my gear quickly and took off, ready for an adventure.

On the second afternoon, while sitting on the deck being warmed by a cup of hot tea, I realized we must be close to the end of the world. The natives on the tiny island of Au, the place we'd chosen to drop anchor, had lived and mated and died on this two-mile stretch of land in the Pacific for generations. They had gotten along quite well without flush toilets, telephones, or dental floss. I was about as far removed from civilization as one can get.

Just as I finished my tea and settled back in the sun ready to listen to the quiet, I began to hear a faint strain of music. Somebody had a radio.

Not wanting to miss a thing, I waited to catch the sound of something authentic and oriental—even the primitive rhythms of a tribe in Borneo. But no, the music sounded vaguely familiar. I strained to catch a few bars. In the middle of nowhere, what was I listening to—again? "Stop—in the name of love, before you break my heart." There on an island in the South China Sea, with not an English-speaking soul around, I was listening to Diana Ross and The Supremes. I could hardly believe my ears. Boomer music, as my kids say.

I had to smile. Our generation has not moved the world the way we thought we would. But we've done a good job of serenading it.

Every generation, I suppose, has its lost ideals—the dreams and myths that gave it momentum and identity. Those who fed on the great expectations and big dreams that accompanied our youth were caught in an interesting paradox.

Due to the sheer size of our numbers, we assumed a place near the center of everyone's attention. Feeling special was normal. But the size of our generation also meant more than feeling special. It meant obscurity. The individual had to shine, and shine brightly, so as not to be lost in the crowd. Out of that paradox was born a tremendous longing for significance. The thought that one might just muddle through life and leave behind little to show for it was totally unappealing. We wanted the world to be different for our having been here. "I want to make my life count" was our rallying cry. Simply put, we wanted to change the world.

I blush now to write those words, half-embarrassed twenty years later that I succumbed to the grandiosity of such idealism. Yet as much as I recognize the naïveté in thinking we could do what other generations tried and failed to accomplish—that we could correct problems centuries old—that longing to make a difference still runs deep. Vestiges of wanting to change the world filter yet through my everyday experience. I feel the weight of personal responsibility to *do* something when I drive by the local juvenile prison and see a sea of fatherless boys from Raleigh's inner city on the basketball court.

Susan looks for a way to derive meaning out of a failed marriage—something she can share with someone else in the same struggle. Grant steadily pursues ways to integrate psychology and theology so that Christianity speaks in relevant language to real needs. Even Ted, who in the middle of shuffling around figures and flowers all day, tries to influence the people who work for him for Christ. Those are some of the ways in which the old dreams persist in our lives, taking different and usually more specific shapes now than they used to.

Big Dreams, Big Disappointments

Our generation grew up looking upon a need as an opportunity—an opportunity with our name on it. War, poverty, prejudice—we lived in a world that needed saving, and still does. For those who were in Sunday school twenty-five years ago—or some version thereof—our solution to the world's problems took a spiritual form. The Great Commission, Christ's departing command to take the gospel to the ends of the earth, provided a way to change the heart of man and, consequently, the world. It was a measurable dream, small increments that added up to a large whole. One person was the key to many more. Between the power of the gospel and a steady supply of adrenalin and eager faces, reaching the world for Christ seemed a doable proposition.

The Great Commission was also a tangible means of making one's life count, a way to rise out of obscurity. Being a small part of a big movement was special. I felt as though I had been let in on a great secret. What could be more exciting than seeing the gospel take hold in another person's life, especially if that person was just one in a chain of future manys? I dismissed things like engagement rings or choosing a major as mere trivialities by comparison. Against a backdrop of reaching the world for Christ, it is easy to understand why our longing for significance was wedded to the concept of size. Here was a dream on the largest scale possible.

The idea of changing the world in one generation calls for big strategies, large armies of man-power, money, and other effective tools. A driving force takes over, and the Great Commission becomes the Great Task to be performed. A giant gospel machine. In striving toward such a huge goal, it becomes difficult to tell whether the individual is the end or the means to the end, or a confusing mix of both.

Here the hope of making a difference, spiritually packaged on a large scale, easily derails; it becomes as much burden as opportunity; it is calcified in global projections. If one person shares the gospel with ten others, there are still twenty more standing right behind them who also need to hear it. There is no end in sight. No matter what you do, the world is never less in need of saving.

Dreams that are so big, so unreachable, tend to dwarf the individual efforts needed to fulfill them. Big is not just better—big is all that really matters. Those kinds of dreams have a disturbing tendency to backfire, for unless you can come up with a way to make sense of your small part, you are destined to be disappointed. When the big dream proves undoable, you are left asking if anyone else missed the train besides you. You are still wondering how to make your life count for something significant.

Perhaps the tale of our generation, as contrasted with our parents', is told in the difference between the soldier of World War II and the one in Vietnam. Our fathers returned from Europe and Asia on top of the world, having liberated entire countries from oppressive dictators and receiving the applause and embraces of fellow Americans for a job well done. But men and women in our generation came back from Vietnam having made the same sacrifice in an unwinnable, highly unpopular war. They received no fanfare, no pats on the back. They got jeers instead of cheers, a homeland with its back turned rather than arms outstretched. Sacrifice lost its aura of nobility. It can be terribly costly, and we learned that sometimes it turns out much differently than you expected.

Vietnam, which was followed by the national embarrassment of Watergate and a presidential resignation, significantly lowered our sights as a generation. All that immense effort had changed our world little. The wheels of power seemed sure to grind steadily onward, and the world no longer appeared as reachable for Christ. So we set out to discover smaller dreams, and the less dramatic, individualized roles we could play in effecting change.

Old Dreams in New Forms

Bittersweet. That word is sometimes used to describe that era of grand and noble dreams. In spite of the fact that we brought about an earlier end to Vietnam, we still lost the war. Maybe the problem of racial inequality got more of the attention it deserved, but basically, the problems remained. The world still needs as much saving now as it did then. We never quite got there, though we are different people, better for all the desire.

Where did all that hunger for meaning and purpose and impact go? What did we do with the disappointment that comes from downscaling such big dreams?

For a long time, it appeared that our generation turned inward and turned sour on outside concerns. We stopped trying so hard to save the world. But media-worn caricatures of our generation as navel-gazing couch potatoes are shortsighted. Our vision may have narrowed and the scope of our concern become more localized, but our longing for impact is still very much intact. It is not dead, but latent—and reemerging with a variety of shapes and characteristics.

LOW-KEY CHANGE AGENTS

When it became harder to make big waves, we developed finer skills in making the smaller ones more effective. We went to work within the very structures we had challenged. Many of the values that marked our earlier ideals are still very much present, flavoring our approach and outlook on society.

Inside the church, where the Pepsi generation and the Harry Truman generation sit in the same pew, change is often slow. Like the ninety-five-year-old lady who said the thing she liked best about her church was that nothing had changed since she was eight years old, ideas about what the church is and what the church should be about are deeply rooted. As the postwar generation has matured and begun to take on positions of leadership, though, the influence of their values—vestiges of earlier dreams—can be felt.

One particular emphasis remains in the necessity of owning your own contribution. Personal responsibility is key. We prefer a stake in the action. Let me do something about a problem rather than just wade through theological debate and endless speculation.

"I'm not content with relegating ministry to the professional," says a man who owns a string of nursing homes in the Northeast. He believes that his job overseeing care for the elderly is as much ministry as it is business. It is not a secondary calling. Half of his clientele is Jewish, and the ethical issues that surround death and dying are everyday fare for him. That is the arena in which he has chosen to live out spiritual realities. "The church doesn't exist to make me feel good," he states. "I'm being fed so that I can do something out there where it counts." This man sees himself as a change agent in a highly specialized setting.

Another way in which the presence of this generation is being felt in the church is in the current emphasis on the relational dimension of the gospel. Our longing for significant relationships has produced an explosion in small groups as opportunities for individuals to connect with other individuals and learn from them. We have wanted models we could learn from, examples of truth fleshed out. Aside from all the verbiage, is there a real person with honest struggles behind the message? We listen closely for the ring of authenticity. It's a value that crops up over and over again.

One middle-aged seminary professor on the West Coast admits that he is emerging from a period where he had grown cynical about Christianity in culture. "I finally realized," he says, "that I was disillusioned with Christianity as it appears in mass form. It's entirely too predictable. It's the public image of organized Christianity that discourages me." What has kept him moving forward has been the "pockets of authentic Christianity." He can cite particular individuals whose lives testify to something real and genuine. Seeing people in small groups who are deeply committed to each other continues to persuade him that real spirituality exists in the context of community.

Hidden under the low-key change agentry to which our big dreams evolved is still the longing to challenge the norm. Beneath the coats and ties, a radical edge lingers. We tend to be uncomfortable with the status quo, willing to rock the boat when necessary.

"At the funniest times I realize that I'm still a refugee of the '60s," explains the chaplain of Duke University, a southern citadel of tradition. The students who come to his office these days are timid, insecure with even the mildest forms of dissent, afraid that a letter urging the board toward divestiture may be too bold. He is in a strange position. He is the establishment now. Yet he finds himself inwardly aghast, wanting to say, "You wimps! Where's your spine?" His wife reminds him when he speaks in chapel that, after all, this is Duke. Perhaps he's being a bit too outspoken, too undignified.

"I take that as a compliment," he says. To him, conflict is just part of the change process, the part that tells him "something's happening."

PATIENCE IN THE PROCESS

One of the improvements in our matured approach to the ideals of our youth is that somewhere in the process, we seem to have acquired a bit of patience. That is another characteristic of the new approach we've given to old dreams.

Nothing much happens quickly—only laxatives work overnight—and slowly but surely, our demand for immediate results has mellowed. Instead of focusing solely on the desired outcome, we have an appreciation for the process of getting there. Not just the arrival, but also the journey takes on significance.

Somewhere in the back of Ted's mind, part of his reason for going into business for himself was the hope of having an impact on the people who worked for him. He saw his business as a platform. In his success, his employees would come to him in search of his spiritual secret, or so he thought.

His story didn't work out that way. He found his failures and setbacks to be humbling, and for a short while, he was tempted to distance himself from his employees. What kind of testimony did he have, anyway? What could he tell them? His life was no great advertisement for a simply-trust-God kind of faith.

Instinctively, though, Ted knew he couldn't live that way. He chose not to hide what was really happening. "I let them share in some of the struggle, offer advice, feel some of the frustration with me. We started to tackle this thing together," Ted explains. He chose to set up a profit-sharing plan during a time when the natural tendency would have been to hang on to every dime.

For ten years, Ted met with two other businessmen one morning a week. There in the back of his store, before the day started, they would spend some time in Bible study, encouraging each other. Ted said little to others about it. He needed the group for his own sanity.

One day, right in the middle of a staff meeting, one of his employees spoke up and challenged Ted. "How come you get with these other men to study the Bible, and you've never offered anything like that to us?" Ted didn't know what to make of that. The men who worked for him were more likely to frequent a happy hour than a Bible study. He had never considered making such a suggestion. One by one they all chimed in. In much the same way that they deliberated over a new marketing plan, they chose a day to begin.

Recently, as Ted was distributing fliers for a design show to all the salesmen, he happened to notice that on each desk, in the middle of the invoices and brochures, lay a *Living Bible*. The sight was a metaphor. "The people who work for us are not the kind who come to Christ and the next day they've cleaned up their act. These people have lived it all," he says. That level of spiritual openness has gone a long way toward making the last five years worth the haul.

By a strange, circuitous route, Ted has found himself in the middle of the kind of ministry he wanted all along— natural and unforced. The best part, he says, is that it wasn't something he orchestrated or sweated blood to make happen. It grew out of the humility of failure and unblanching honesty. It grew out of patience.

There is something redeeming about having to take the long way around sometimes. You get the benefit of hindsight. You get to see all the seemingly small things that added up to more than you would have thought. And you come away with the sense that much of what is truly significant rarely *feels* that way at the time.

JOY IN THE GENUINE

We didn't change the world. We didn't even come close. What has changed, in fact, has been the shape of our original longings.

It's hard to reach the world with a two-year-old cling- ing to your skirt. You can't rewrite nuclear policy and still get your marketing plan done by Friday. The course of Western civilization probably won't be altered by your re- search dissertation on Carl Jung. The big dreams get bro- ken up into smaller pieces the way phrases are broken by dashes and commas in a sentence.

The great numbers and longitudinal projections have evolved into something relational and fluid, more like con- centric circles than geometric lines and pyramids. We seem to have traded our affinity for the large and showy for a deeper experience of the genuine. I asked a woman re- cently why she continued, week after week, to hold recov- ery groups for women who had had abortions. Her answer spoke for many people making little contributions in soup kitchens and homeless shelters, or among drug-addicted teenagers and the declining elderly. "I found that in this group I was perched right on the edge of watching the deepest truths of the gospel take root in one of the most hidden of all secrets—that of allowing the life of your own child to be taken," she said. In other words, she was able to participate in the changed lives of a few individuals, and that was both enough and a lot. What happens beyond that point, only God knows.

On my summer trip overseas, I happened to squeeze two totally different experiences into the same day. The contrast between them was a parable of sorts.

In Singapore I went out shopping for the day and found myself on Orchard Road. I had only vaguely heard of Orchard Road, but in short order I realized I was in a shopper's paradise. Gucci and Christian Dior and Rolex, silks, laces, jewelry, and electronics—a sampling of everything made in the world was for sale here. The dazzle, the spectacle before me pumped up my adrenaline, and before too many hours had passed, I had spent my little wad. The experience was exhilarating. Yet I came home feeling bone tired and about as plastic as my charge card.

The same evening Stacy and I met with a group of Indian couples who had asked us to talk about what we were learning about marriage in midlife. Though we had never met them before, though their culture, accent and dress, and the color of their skin were all different from our own, I was instantly aware of feeling right at home. There was an immediacy of connection with them, a warmth and ease in their presence that one could only explain as the Lord. Yet it was a simple evening. Nothing extraordinary took place. We discussed the struggles and frustrations, the unexpected pleasures of living with the same person for fifteen years or so. The delight I found was the simple thrill of taking part in others' lives—and of being touched by their involvement in mine.

I realized that I had spent too many years looking for the Orchard Roads of the Christian life. My craving for the momentous had almost spoiled me for being able to appreciate the joy in the ordinary. My attachment to big dreams had blinded me to those little, unpredictable, incandescent moments with people when what is experienced is nothing less than the life of God in us and between us.

I'm not sure when it finally dawned on me that if you took everything my life was about, it still wouldn't add up to all that much. Or that all my efforts would never bring me a permanent fix of significance and meaning. Or that if I continued to measure the worth of my life by what it had accomplished, I would be in trouble. I'm only glad it did.

I still long to see the world change. But I've grown much more content with my small contribution. The guilt of not doing it all rests lighter on my shoulders. Though I have the same heart, I have narrowed my field. Or as Madeleine L'Engle says in one of her poems:

> To grow up
> is to find
> the small part you are playing
> in this extraordinary drama
> written by
> Somebody else.[1]

What I know now, but I didn't
know then, is that there are no secrets or short cuts to growing up.

Cheryl Merser, 39

12

Fresh Starts

Embracing a Realistic Hope

J ust inside the entrance of a retreat center in the Valley of Virginia, four similar paintings hang together as a group. The subject is simple. In each painting there is a boat with a sole occupant heading down a river toward the lights of a city in the distance. It is the progression that tells the story.

The artist intends to let you see the classic passages of life through visual metaphor. In the first painting, a baby sleeps in the vessel as the smooth current carries the boat gently along. The second picture depicts a rugged young man standing in the rear of the boat, the steering wheel firmly within his grip and his eyes fixed on the bright lights of a distant city. He is strong and capable and in control, heading resolutely toward his goal.

The third painting tells another story. The water churns like rapids in a deep river gorge, spraying fine mists over the side of the boat. A low-lying fog obscures the lights of that once-bright city, and the captain of this ship is no longer young and no longer standing. His hands are nowhere near the steering wheel. He's on his knees in the back of the boat hanging on for dear life, a look of distress on his face.

The last picture is the best of all. An old man, slightly worn around the edges, sits peacefully in the boat with his hand lightly resting on the wheel. Neither lines of resignation nor of striving crease his cheeks. He is at ease. The years have taught him to relax and trust the boat and current to carry him.

Those paintings hold a viewer's attention because they give an overview of a journey we are all taking. They are four distinct stages in life, four passages common to a normal life span. If you identify with the man in the third painting—not old but no longer young—there is something comforting about recognizing the flux and confusion, the panic and disappointment, for the common responses that they are.

For our generation, those responses are almost automatic, given our backgrounds. For us who count ourselves among the generation born to parents elated by the victory of World War II, our transition—from idealistic youth seeking our own bright vistas, to sobered, middle-aged adults often overwhelmed with life—has been much harder. We have known a rougher-than-normal passage.

If you find yourself somewhere in this process of negotiating your way through the middle of life, there is some encouraging news. Most transitions, especially midlife, follow three fairly predictable stages.[1] The first is probably the hardest. An inner restlessness begins to call for change, but it's not clear what kind or how much. It may feel as though you've outgrown the place you're in, as if your particular role or task no longer fits you.

When you find yourself in this phase of disenchantment, what you need to look for is some time to reassess, to sort out, to look for what may be missing. Ironically, what has aided you up to this point—your self-image, style of relating, approach to a task—may hinder you from the growth that is called for now. What got you this far may not take you where you want to go. Ted, for instance, spent the first half of his life as a lone ranger, accustomed to battling against the odds by sheer force of individual determination. But his business difficulties forced him to take a mental "time out." He realized that he needed a more participatory approach to work. He needed to learn how to draw out someone else's talents.

The second stage is called the neutral zone. This is a fallow period, sometimes painful, more often just flat and shapeless. The tendency here is to rush out and try a quick fix or to push yourself through to the next phase. But it is the person who gives himself time and space who experiences real renewal. To just push down the inner issues and go on when those issues needed to surface is to find they come up again later—with added wallop. Those who take the time to regroup now come out stronger in the end.

Eventually, the neutral zone gives way to a new beginning. Your energy and zest return; some new venture or way of relating beckons, and you are able to move forward. "The lesson of all such experiences is that when we are ready to make a beginning, we will shortly find an opportunity."[2]

Part of growing up, in the fuller sense of the word, is learning how to make sense of your own journey. It means recognizing your expectations and digesting your disappointments. It is coming to terms with life as it is as well as how it ought to be. It is letting go and moving on with hope, not resignation.

Riding Looser in the Saddle

For many people, the decade between ages thirty-five and forty-five is marked by mini-losses, by a sense of dissatisfaction, by the struggle to turn dreams into reality. Somewhere along the way it's easy to lose sight of the opportunity we're being offered. There are gains as well as losses. The hidden wealth in disappointed dreams is that we are offered the chance to lay hold of a new approach to life.

Susan knows that experiencing a failed marriage, although she would never have wished for it, has nevertheless built a resilience and depth in her that wasn't there before. She has not only survived divorce, she has grown through the pain. "It's one thing to believe in yourself at twenty," she says. "But when you've survived a broken world experience and even overcome in places, then you start to believe there's something of serious substance there."

Susan's divorce has also changed her relationships for the better. "I feel less need for a fantasy person, less need to idealize other people," she explains. She can recognize their gifts and abilities, their special competencies, but their mixed motivations and internal struggles are no longer a mystery to her. In her relationship with God, she experiences a reciprocity that wasn't there before. She feels freedom to interact, confident that if she gives something time, the truth will rise to the surface.

Susan is the first to admit that she lives in the daily reminders of unfulfilled longings. There are gaps in her girls' experience that leave her with the same old ache. No matter how hard she tries, she can't be both father and mother. Between her children's needs and her own, she is often tired and worn out, feeling at times as though her greatest parenting accomplishment is that she "showed up." Yet she feels the quiet satisfaction of living out her faith in circumstances that fall short of anyone's ideal.

Once you've made it through some significant disappointments, new ones lose a little of their sting. You can be disappointed without being devastated. The person who is disappointed prepares to weather the crisis; the one who is devastated doubts that he can. Part of the hidden gift to the person who has faced crisis and survived is that he rides more loosely in the saddle from that point forward. He is not wasting bundles of energy braced and tense, working overtime to keep his carefully constructed dreams from crashing about his feet. His hands are no longer gripped, white-knuckled around the reins.

Freer of Illusions

What the disenchantment of our dreams also does for us is to shake us free from many of our illusions about life. We are *dis-illusioned,* and although that word has a negative connotation, the process is decidedly positive. It's a key ingredient, a necessary part of what it means to embrace reality.

Part of the baggage of youth is the half-formed idea that real life will begin at the next juncture in the road. Just around the corner. Somewhere out there, a bright tomorrow holds the completion that eludes you today. When you are single and twenty-five, marriage is the answer to what ails you. Or, it's a good job. Then you have a few children. You buy a house and settle down. But each new step fails to bring you any closer, really, to the end of the rainbow. You can't seem to reach the place where all the jagged pieces of life fit into a whole.

Growing up means facing that small, incessant ache in your own soul and realizing that it will never go away in this life. It wasn't meant to.

Grant thought that moving to the suburbs where he could establish his own practice was the event he'd been waiting for. But when this bright future of tomorrow actually became today and the aura faded, he discovered he was pretty much the same guy with a new set of problems. "There wasn't any more real peace and sanity here than there had been in the city," he says. "I wasn't living on easy street."

The illusion he was forced to let go of was the idea of "the perfect life." There was no fixed set of variables that he could get all lined up at the same time that would baptize his life with "happiness." And with that deep realization, he found unexpected freedom. "I've seen what a joke it is to think I could finally come upon the key to a perfect life," he says. "Once I let go of that illusion, I find I'm enjoying life in the present in a new way—my kids, my marriage, my patients, me." He feels able to live in the confusion and ambiguity of it all without his old frantic, perfectionistic tendencies to Do It Right.

But he has not given up on his dreams. He continues to piece together, bit by bit, a kind of "liberation theology of the soul." He believes that the church is on the verge of a second reformation, a new attempt to allow Christianity to speak to the real needs of modern man. He'd like to be there with a model, a blending of psychology and theology that will work. But at this point, he is not living in suspended animation until his dreams materialize.

Grant's illusion of the perfect life is a common myth that any of us can fall for. It is just one of many false hopes we let go of in order to grow.

Embracing Life

In Madeleine L'Engle's trilogy of journals she writes about her maternal grandmother, Mado, a Southern lady who lost her husband at a young age and lived through years of poverty in the Reconstruction days of the South. She describes Mado as an old woman with that "peculiar quality of aliveness" that comes to people who have already done a lot of their dying.[3] It intrigues me that vibrancy of life should be connected to loss and dying dreams. The two would appear contradictory. But there is freedom in letting go, in dying to some of our false hopes. We begin to realize that we can't control the world—not even our own world. It is a humbling recognition that actually brings relief.

In the middle of life is where we come to an invisible fork in the road. We can either try to reduce the scope of our world size that *appears* controllable, or we can take a wide and risky, energizing step. We can refuse the temptation to batten down the hatches and, instead, open ourselves to receive the people and experiences that come our way. We can trade certainty for adventure, and in the process come alive in a new way. Like Steve Martin in the movie *Parenthood*, we learn to laugh more on the roller coaster and enjoy the ride.

Accepting life as it is, in some ways, is an even greater feat than realizing your dreams. Says one friend, "In my family we always called this kind of person a 'maintainer,' and we kind of sneered when we said the word. But I have come to see that acceptance can be a strong, magnificent thing—something that Jesus Himself had to do." Making peace with life as it is can be as noble as reaching for the stars, as great as John Wayne taking the West. It's as much a part of life as realizing all your best hopes.

That is how dying dreams can give birth to something better, to that paradoxical quality of "aliveness" that characterized Madeleine L'Engle's grandmother. Embracing life as it is releases you to experience what is actually before you. Mere life can hold fresh joy. Lesser, at times, becomes mysteriously more.

Part of the freedom at this point in life is the potential to give to others without strings attached. That is what developmental theorists call generativity.[4] Some of that energy to prove yourself is rechanneled into a capacity to mentor others and to bring them along with you. Many people believe that is the path to replenishment in the middle of life. In the freedom of not having to push ahead, when that do-or-die compulsion subsides, then we are able to invest in others for their sakes. We no longer look at someone else as an extension of ourselves or as a means toward our own all-important end.

That is what Ted discovered when his business didn't take off the way he had hoped it would. For a long time, all he saw was the goals he would probably never reach. What stood out was his own failure to achieve the kind of success for which he'd hoped. He almost missed the really special things that were happening around him because he was so busy looking for something else.

"I finally got to the point where I could see there was something blossoming around me, and it was people. The pleasure shifted focus. Helping these guys who worked with me feel an ownership in what they were doing, watching them develop, these were the things that seemed to matter—as much as creating a big, successful company had in the past," he says.

More and more, there is a note of sheer gratefulness that comes out in Ted's reflections on their last five years. His children have learned a lot, they've been able to keep their house, his business is now making slow, steady gains, a few of his employees have found Christ. "The goodness of God is what stands out to me these days—that He doesn't want or need anything from us, that He never, never lets us go."

Gratitude

I recently read an interview with Sylvester Stallone, the forty-three-year-old "Rocky" who turns to painting when he is not acting. His life impresses me as one that models the general angst of our generation. Somewhere in each of his paintings is the picture of a clock. He owns thirty watches and rarely sleeps the night through. It's a waste of time, he says. He sees his strength, his youth, his time slipping past him. He is driven to find that mythical point where all his dreams converge and crystallize and leave him dazzled by their brilliance.

We may not be that obsessed with time, but most of us know what it's like to hear the encroachment of age clicking like a metronome in our ears.

When a person has faced his dreams head-on, however, when he has been forced to reshape a few and let go of others, then the passage of time is not so threatening. He is not looking for an event to give him meaning. It's not later when I get my Ph.D. or build a house or establish a home for unwed mothers. It is life as it happens now, right under my nose.

This newfound ability to enjoy life as it is leads to a quiet sense of gratitude. And perhaps gratitude is what you least expect to feel after wading through a time of finding new shapes to old dreams. I found that it snuck up on me from behind when I least suspected it.

I first noticed gratitude in the form of lightness. It's amazing how your dreams can become such burdens. To be more relieved of the need to do something remarkable is freedom. When your life doesn't always have to be validated by some external source, you can begin to enjoy it so much more. It's striking how much simple pleasure there is in relationships when your children and your spouse do not feel the unspoken pressure to compensate for your unrealized expectations of life.

"Some luck lies in not getting what you thought you wanted," wrote Garrison Keillor, "but getting what you have which once you have it you may be smart enough to see is what you would have wanted all along had you known."[5] You no longer have to force your life into a prearranged shape to be happy. You are less afraid to lose, less encumbered.

What makes that feeling of gratefulness even more unexpected is all the anger and frustration, the sense of loss which preceded it. We would so prefer to go around—not through—that kind of emotional territory, though perhaps it is more necessary than we realize.

Last fall I helped my parents pack up thirty-five years of life in the same home—a house they built right after the war—so they could move to a smaller place without an acre of lawn to mow.

On the last day I took a break and sneaked off to sit on the swing that had hung for years beneath a huge old oak tree in the yard. That tree has presided, a silent, towering figure, over all the doings of our family. After World War II, a young couple had cleared the virgin land around this tree and left it standing while their home was being built. Children had spent long summer nights catching lightning bugs, and, later, wedding receptions were celebrated beneath its boughs. This was certainly one place where I had formed many of my own hopes for life.

In the last few years, my children had used its barnacled trunk as a base for their games of Hide and Seek. And now, I realized, other families and other generations of children would grow up and live out their lives right here, under the shade of this old tree. The most obvious thought struck me, all the more forcefully because I had lived on top of it all these years. I was now, and always had been, only a *visitor.*

It was one of those moments when I could stand back and see the bigger picture. I could see what a small place I occupied in the overall scheme of things. There is no room to demand that life go my way, that it unfold according to my preconceived notions. The world is not my oyster. I'm not going to be here forever. That experience left me a bit more grateful for the small, special pleasures that come my way.

A Realistic Hope

We said we'd never grow up and we'd never grow old; we'd never trust anyone over thirty. And now most of us have long since passed that tender age and are in the midst of giving each other black fortieth birthday parties. Who knows? We may yet grow old.

For our generation, more than any other in this century, the twenty-five years between youth and middle-age have been marked by unmet expectations. We found many of our dreams unreachable. Growing up has been less about realizing our dreams and more about making our dreams subject to reality.

In one sense, when we tied our faith to our cultural expectations, we succumbed to the illusion that we could experience heaven in the here and now. It is true that one day our dreams and longings will be fulfilled beyond our wildest imaginations. Life will happen the way it's supposed to, the way we always wanted it to—someday—*but not now.* Now we plow through time, groping, learning, hurting, struggling, failing, and sometimes succeeding. God can help us and strengthen us, but He never promised to keep us from pain. "Our Father refreshes us with some pleasant inns on the journey, but [he] will not encourage us to mistake them for home," wrote C. S. Lewis.[6] No matter what the song says, heaven is not a place on earth.

Perhaps disappointed dreams are our best opportunities to transfer hope to its rightful place. Heaven is where our biggest dreams belong. Realizing that can help us make it through the here and now without placing a burden on the present that it was never meant to bear. That's hope—realistic hope—which may yet serve to carry us through the rest of the journey.

Study Guide

by William D. Watkins

Chapter 1: An Invitation

1. Let your mind wander back to your younger years, when you were between five and twelve years old. Then push your memories ahead to your teenage years. In each of those periods of your life, what experiences, events, or beliefs shaped your understanding of the world around you? In what ways do these factors still influence your life? Record your reflections in the chart below.

MY CHILDHOOD	PAST INFLUENCES	PRESENT IMPACT
Ages 5–12		
Ages 13–19		

2. When you were a pre–twenty–year–old, what age was old—over the hill—to you? Why did you think this?

_____

_____

Is there an age that seems too old now? Why or why not?

_____

_____

3. Have you reached a point where you think of yourself as "older than young," where you realize you are middle-aged? When did this realization first hit you? How do you feel about growing older?

_____

_____

_____

4. When we were kids, we all had dreams. Maybe it was to become a great architect or a highly respected physician or a popular movie star. Or perhaps it was to change the world's political landscape or bring peace to a war-torn world or create world-renowned art and literature or be the star performer in a world-famous rock band. If you connected your dreams with an all-powerful God who was always on your side and would never let you experience much (or any!) pain or failure, you may even have added to your dream list playing a significant role in world evangelization or some other religious quest. Below, take a few minutes to record your childhood dreams, then note if they came true, even for just a short period of time.

MY CHILDHOOD DREAMS	THEIR FULFILLMENT

5. Do you sense disappointment in your life—an emptiness or lack that won't go away? Is it tied to unfulfilled dreams? If so, which ones?

_____

_____

_____

_____

_____

_____

Or maybe your expectations about life have been realized, at least mostly, and yet you still feel as if something is amiss. Can you identify what's wrong?

_____

_____

_____

_____

_____

Chapter 2: Less Than We Bargained For

In the previous chapter, we helped you focus on your past and present in general terms, getting a kind of bird's-eye view. Here we want to provide you with an opportunity to get more specific, even more personal. We want you to look more deeply into what you feel about your life and explore why you have those feelings.

1. Consider the following quotes from chapter 2, then put a check mark under the response that best fits with how you believe these quotes apply to your life.

QUOTES	STRONGLY AGREE	SOMEWHAT AGREE	UNDECIDED	SOMEWHAT DISAGREE	STRONGLY DISAGREE
"Underneath all my busyness, I find I am mostly just very tired, and a bit bewildered with my life." (p. 27)					
"We are . . . 'the sandwich generation,' caught between competing demands and desires." (p. 27)					
"We are grownups still in search of that inner sense of being fully adult." (p. 29)					
"We often appear to be doing better than we actually are." (p. 29)					
"Most of the time I'm just spinning around in circles, carrying out a list of tasks, connected to no one." (p. 34)					
"Loneliness is a persistent struggle for me." (p. 36)					
"I feel that there's a life I was raised to have, and financially I just haven't been able to make that happen." (pp. 36–37)					
"Divorce and business failures, insecurity and dissatisfaction, were not part of our mental concept of the abundant life in Christ." (p. 40)					

2. If most of your check marks landed on the "strongly agree" or "somewhat agree" columns of the above chart, you certainly feel as though you have gotten less than you bargained for. Your life's expectations have not matched your life's realities. You are disappointed, probably frustrated and somewhat confused, maybe even hurt and angry. What did you expect adulthood to be like? How is adulthood actually turning out? Make your answers as specific as you can.

MY GREAT EXPECTATIONS	MY NOT-SO-GREAT REALIZATIONS

3. We saw that even though Grant was highly respected in his chosen career of psychology, his self-doubts created within him fear and anxiety. Moreover, the stresses imposed by his career were taking a toll on his ability to set aside time to catch his breath and reflect on where he's going and why. We also saw how Ted began a floral business, prospered, then held on while it nose-dived when bad economic times hit his area. Then we read about Susan. We heard how she went into her marriage with Jim expecting to find security and happiness. Now she's divorced, the single parent of two children, and constantly battling with fatigue and loneliness.

Can you identify with any of these people? Do you seem to be at the top of your form to everyone else but yourself? Are your relationships not what you had hoped they would be? Are you overworked, underpaid, and wobbling under a heavy load of responsibilities? Is the achievement of your dreams being threatened by your finances? Do you find it hard to find God in all of this? Do you wonder how your struggles, your heartaches, your weariness relate to the abundant life promised in Christ? Take some time to pour out your thoughts and feelings. Don't worry about what others might think or say. Just be honest—at least to yourself. God knows how you feel anyway, so let it out.

_____

_____

_____

_____

_____

_____

_____

_____

_____

_____

_____

_____

_____

_____

_____

_____

_____

Now that you've got this down on paper, ask God to help you continue to get in touch with how you feel, what you think, and why. In order to deal with that gnawing sense of disappointment looming below the surface of your life, you need to be able to identify what's causing it and why. Since God knows us better than we know ourselves, the sooner we get Him involved in the process, the better it will go. Don't get me wrong. I'm not saying the process will get easier—it may even become harder. But the Lord will stay by your side, and He'll help bring to the light those things that desperately need to be exposed and dealt with.

Chapter 3: The Children of Promise

1. Paula Rinehart described an event out of her past that capsulized her assumptions about life—what she believed life was like and what it would provide for her (pp. 43–44). Is there an event from your past that sums up what your childhood expectations of life were? Describe the experience and what assumptions it reveals to you.

_____

_____

_____

_____

_____

_____

_____

_____

_____

2. There's no doubt that our parents' growing-up experiences were much different from ours and that their experiences shaped them as much as ours shaped us. In the chart below, you will have the opportunity to list world events (e.g., world wars, world-wide financial booms or busts), cultural events (e.g., presidential assassinations, TV shows, birth rates), and upbringing events (e.g., parents who were too permissive or too strict, being taught that people could do anything they put their minds and muscle to) that shaped your parents' life perspective and behavior. Then you'll have the chance to do the same for yourself. Through this exercise, you'll gain a visual picture of contrasts that will help you see how different you and your generation are from your parents and their generation and why those differences exist.

	MY PARENTS' PAST	MY PAST
Shaping World Events		
Shaping Cultural Events		
Shaping Upbringing Events		

3. In the next chart, record what your parents' past taught them about what they could expect from life, then do the same for yourself. If you have never spoken to your parents about this, you may want to give them a call or visit them and ask them about it. If that's not possible, you may still have a good feel for how their past shaped their life view. Just recall their disappointments, their attitudes, their advice, their instruction, and any other telltale indicators. You will likely piece together a fairly accurate portrait.

MY PARENTS' LIFE VIEW	MY LIFE VIEW

4. As you reflect on the answers you put down in the two previous charts, what key similarities do they point out between you and your parents?

_____

_____

_____

_____

What are the important differences?

_____

_____

_____

_____

In which generation would you have rather lived—yours or your parents'? Why?

_____

_____

_____

Does this comparison suggest ways in which you might want to reshape your life view? If so, what would you change?

_____

_____

_____

5. As Paula Rinehart points out, in 1967 *Time* magazine wrote about the Baby-Boom Generation: "In its lifetime, this promising generation could land on the moon, cure cancer and the common cold, lay out blight-proof, smog-free cities, help end racial prejudice, enrich the underdeveloped world, and, no doubt, write an end to poverty and war" (p. 53). If you had read that appraisal in 1967, would you have agreed with it?

_____

What do you think about it now?

_____

_____

_____

If the answer you would give now differs from what you would have said in 1967, explain what has changed your mind.

_____

_____

_____

6. In question 1, you described an event from your past that summarized your childhood assumptions about life. Now pick an event from your adulthood, preferably one that occurred just before or during your middle-aged years, that conveys in a nutshell what you now think and feel about life.

_____

_____

_____

_____

_____

_____

_____

What do the differences between these two events tell you about how your life perspective has changed?

_____

_____

_____

_____

Chapter 4: Broken Rainbows

1. It's uncomfortable and disconcerting to search your mind and heart and realize that you're disappointed, perhaps even angry, with God. You may not feel that way right now, or maybe you did at one time but you've worked through it and put it behind you. One thing is certain: If you're honest with yourself, at some point in your life you will feel as though God has let you down. It's a universal problem. The Old Testament saints experienced it, and so did the New Testament believers. In fact, Christians throughout the centuries have struggled with this issue.

Think back through the biblical record and see how many Old Testament or New Testament believers you can recall who felt that God had frustrated their expectations. Also jot down the focus of their disappointment; for example, a feeling that God abandoned them, unjust treatment by others, divine grace exercised on unbelievers when wrath was expected, being harshly treated by enemies or even by God, or failing at a task when they expected God to give them success.

DISAPPOINTMENT WITH GOD IN SCRIPTURE

THE BIBLE CHARACTERS	THE DISAPPOINTMENT'S FOCUS

2. Paula Rinehart mentions several contemporary people who thought God had promised them a certain kind of life, only to find out that God never made those promises. Consider the "promises" that follow and indicate whether you believed (or still believe) them.

FALSE PROMISES	"I USED TO BELIEVE THEM"	"I BELIEVE THEM NOW"	"I NEVER BELIEVED THEM"
(1) Since God loves me and has a wonderful plan for my life, no serious harm can come to me.			
(2) The Bible will show me the right path to follow in everything, so I will never make a wrong decision.			
(3) God guarantees unfailing success to those who are faithful to Him.			
(4) God will protect me from serious financial problems.			
(5) If I do what's right, I will always be treated right.			
(6) If I'm a loving, faithful spouse, my mate will never leave me.			
(7) If I parent my children according to God's principles, they will never get into serious problems or leave the faith.			

Are there any other false promises you would like to add to this list? Cite them here.

_____

_____

_____

_____

3. How do we know these are promises God never made, even though some people claimed He did and we believed them? What Scriptures or biblical stories tip you off that these promises are bogus?

_____

_____

_____

_____

_____

4. Most false beliefs are mixed with elements of truth. Are there any elements of truth in the above promises? In other words, could they be modified in any way to express legitimate promises, or at least principles that are generally, though not always, true?

Revised promise 1: _____

_____

Revised promise 2: _____

_____

Revised promise 3: _____

_____

Revised promise 4: _____

_____

Revised promise 5: _____

_____

Revised promise 6: _____

_____

Revised promise 7: _____

_____

5. The fallout of embracing false promises is false guilt, false pretenses, and false contracts. Have you ever experienced these problems? How have you dealt with them?

_____

_____

_____

_____

_____

How can acknowledging the promises God never made help you deal with these fallout issues?

_____

_____

_____

_____

Chapter 5: Rude Awakenings

1. A rude awakening is an unexpected happening "that dislodges some of our most valued dreams, throwing us off balance. . . . For the person who is 'rudely awakened,' there is an inner sense of being stopped short, of wanting to ask, 'Hey, what's going on here? My life is not unfolding the way I thought it would'" (pp. 69–70). If you have had an experience that fits this description, recount it here and explain what personal beliefs and values it upset.

_____

_____

_____

_____

_____

2. Perhaps your maturation from young adulthood to middle age was not marked by a rude awakening but by slow dawnings. As Paula Rinehart describes it, "One day folds into the next, another deadline is met, and there is little time to reflect. . . . Little by little, you just sense your life evolving into something different than you imagined. Sometimes, a feeling of stagnation, disequilibrium, or mild depression sets in. The results of earlier choices become plain, yet not easily reversed. Options seem to have narrowed, but responsibilities have grown" (p. 73).

What shape did your slow dawnings take? What changes have they brought in your beliefs and values?

_____

_____

_____

_____

_____

_____

3. Paula Rinehart describes three illusions that are shattered by rude awakenings and slow dawnings. In your own words, describe each one and explain how, if at all, each one has been cornered and challenged in your life.

The illusion of success: _____

_____

_____

_____

The illusion of control: _____

_____

_____

_____

The illusion of exemption: _____

_____

_____

_____

4. By this point, you may be seeing some of the hidden wealth in your disappointed dreams—that is, you may have begun to discover that your frustrations, hurts, and struggles through midlife do have a positive payoff. Although you're going to be exploring this fact more thoroughly throughout the rest of the book, take a few moments now to recount some of the treasures you may have already discovered.

_____

_____

_____

_____

_____

_____

Chapter 6: Inner Spaces

"When a significant aspect of a person's outer world is shaken, a quieter hidden process begins on the inside as well. . . . [This] shift in focus is a God-given opportunity to take a personal inventory of our lives. . . . It is a chance to reassess, to sink our personal roots down into what is really true about ourselves, our relationships, our faith, our lives" (p. 83).

To this point in your study, you have dealt a lot with events and experiences and their impact on your life. In other words, you have worked through a number of external factors and tried to get a handle on how they have shaken you, your beliefs, your values, your life perceptions. From here on, the focus is going to shift; it will become more internally oriented. You'll be dealing with matters of the heart: "Our real self, a sense of inner home, the place where we experience the closest, most direct contact with the presence of God" (p. 85). Here is where the toughest, and yet greatest, long-lasting work begins. Here is found the finest treasure. Let's get started.

    1. We've all seen teenagers go through identity crises. And almost all of us experienced it ourselves at some point in our teen years or early twenties. But did you know that your thirties or forties would lead to another identity crisis? The central issue is still the same: "Who am I?" But what brings the question to the forefront has changed. It's not the need for independence from parents, rather it's the need for independence from being defined by what we do and how others perceive us. It is no easy task. The layers we must peel away are many and thick. They've been building up for a long time, like the delta at the mouth of the Mississippi River.

    You can see this for yourself with a little reflection. Think of the many people in your life and consider how they view you. Don't they usually define you in terms of the roles you play—the functions or jobs you perform—especially in their lives? In the chart below, list the people in your life (parents, children, employer, co-workers, clients, friends, neighbors), the roles you play for them (confidant, nurse, information gatherer, problem solver, financial supplier) and the way they see you; then notice the correlations between your roles and the way you are perceived.

THE PEOPLE IN MY LIFE	THE ROLES I PLAY FOR THEM	THE WAY THEY SEE ME

2. Now consider how you *want* to be perceived. When people meet you and get to know you, what do you want them to believe about you? What image are you trying to project?

_____

_____

_____

3. Now for the most important matter of all: How much does your image truly reflect who you really are? Does your exterior match your interior? Does your performance-based identity square with your internal reality?

You may have never really dealt with this issue before. It may feel uncomfortable, perhaps even painful. That's OK. Take your time. Maybe even talk it over with someone close to you, someone who will shoot straight with you and yet be gentle and kind. But remember, a critical step to self-authenticity is self-honesty. Admitting that differences between our external and internal identities exist and pinpointing those differences can go far in helping us resolve our identity crises. So don't avoid the issue because it might bring some pain. Go slowly if you must, but don't fail to go.

_____

_____

_____

_____

4. Growing older, shifting images of self, and disappointment in others all fuel a search for authenticity. In what ways, if at all, have these three factors moved you toward self-reevaluation and reorientation?

For me growing older has _____

_____

_____

For me shifting self images has _____

_____

_____

For me disappointment in others has _____

_____

_____

Chapter 7: Becoming Real

1. In the last chapter, we looked at the roles we play for others and how they influence the way people perceive us. Although we don't want to be defined simply—or even primarily—in terms of what we do, we must realize that each of us is called by God to play a role He has designed for us. And our role is intimately connected with who we are as individuals. Consequently, the search for self-authenticity leads to the discovery of our God-given calling.

The Son of God understands this. When He came to earth and took on a human nature so He could fulfill the Father's will, He had to combat the expectations and perceptions of others. He didn't come to liberate the Jews from Roman rule or reform political institutions or heal everyone from every physical ailment or make the impoverished financially wealthy. His mission was to teach and model the gospel, to die on a cross for human sin, and to rise from the dead in victory over death so that all who trust in Him by faith could be saved to enjoy God forever. Because He fulfilled His calling, the Father exalted Him above every other name.

What is *your* calling? Is it to teach in a public or private school? Is it to conduct research? Is it to sing, program computers, raise children, preach, develop or manage a business venture, or create art? Perhaps you're unsure of your calling, or maybe you've lost touch with it. Give the matter some thought and commit it to prayer, trusting that the Lord will help you identify it and fulfill it as you trust in Him. As it becomes clear to you, record it here and ask God to help it sink deep roots in your life so that it will eventually nourish and shape everything you do and become.

_____

_____

_____

_____

2. One of the hidden fortunes in disappointment is "a new ability to live within your limitations" (p. 98). Have you ever felt that you had to be good at everything? Since we are limited by nature, the temptation of omnicompetence is a vicious, pressure-filled trap for us. Only God is omnicompetent, and the sooner we realize that, the better off we'll be—in fact, we'll taste the sweetness of a freedom we have never known before.

What steps can you start taking this week to accept your limitations and begin living within them? Be as specific as you can.

_____

_____

_____

_____

3. Another hidden wealth in disappointed dreams is "a deeper ability to love others. . . . When we are uncomfortable with who we are, when our emotional survival depends on keeping our idealized image intact, we are not free to love. Our energies are siphoned off by the task of protecting that image. We peek around at each other from behind a thousand masks, trying to escape the risk of letting someone into the inner circle of our lives" (pp. 101–2). Does that describe you? In what ways do you protect your self-image and in the process cut yourself off from opportunities for greater intimacy?

_____

_____

_____

_____

How can you become more comfortable with yourself so that you can channel more of your energy into loving others rather than in simply or mainly protecting yourself?

_____

_____

_____

_____

_____

(If you come from an abusive past, self-protection will understandably be high on your list of priorities. Learning to trust others will not be easy. It's also true, though, that if your walls of self-protection have no gates that allow people in from time to time, you will never enjoy the kind of intimacy with others God longs for you to have. So even though it may be scary, take some occasional risks. Keep them small at first to allow your self-confidence and trust to grow, but don't leave the gates locked to everyone. You can't lock out fear or hurt no matter what you do; however, you *can* lock out intimacy and love by keeping the gates to your heart shut to all outsiders.)

4. Another benefit of disappointment is discovering "an inner resilience we did not know we possessed" (p. 103). Have you faced fears or hurts you never thought you would survive but made it through them anyway? If so, recount such an instance here, and tell what you learned about yourself, life, and God.

_____

_____

_____

_____

_____

_____

_____

_____

Chapter 8: Loose Connections

1. When you dreamed about the perfect relationship in your younger days, what did it look like?

_____

_____

_____

Now that you've pursued your dream relationship, what do you think about it? Is it a realistic, achievable dream? Does it need some revision? If so, what would your truer-to-life relationship look like now?

_____

_____

2. Why have we found it hard to create a thriving, satisfying relationship with another person? Paula Rinehart lists several reasons. Check off the ones that may apply to you, then feel free to add any others that especially pertain to your situation.

REASONS FOR RELATIONAL MISCONNECTIONS	"I CAN RELATE"	"THAT DOESN'T APPLY TO MY SITUATION"
(1) Personal past baggage		
(2) The elusive nature of intimacy		
(3) Unresolved issues in the relationship itself		
(4) The different rhythms of the male and female achieving and nurturing drives		
(5) Our own worst fears		
(6) Everyday stress and strains		
(7) _____		

3. In light of these hurdles to intimacy, why go to all the effort to strive to achieve it? On pages 110–19 you'll find some reasons. See if you can pick them out; then feel free to add some of your own. We're trying to help you build a case for seeking to deepen your relationships, even when you feel like giving up or running away. This way you can find adequate reasons to keep moving ahead rather than retreating in defeat.

Reason 1: _____

Reason 2: _____

Reason 3: _____

Reason 4: _____

Reason 5: _____

Reason 6: _____

Reason 7: _____

4. Whether you're married or not, you likely have at least one relationship that you would like to deepen. List three things you can put into practice this week that could help you achieve that goal. These are not magic steps to greater intimacy, but they are steps you can build on to develop a deeper, stronger relationship.

Step 1: _____

_____

_____

Step 2: _____

_____

_____

Step 3: _____

_____

_____

Chapter 9: Making It

1. When you were growing up, what was your picture of the good life? Did it include a nice house complete with children, pets, a loving spouse, a thriving career, and a car that would be everyone's envy? Describe the good life as you defined it in your youth.

_____

_____

_____

_____

Has your vision of the good life changed over the years? If so, what does the good life look like now?

_____

_____

_____

_____

2. Do you think you have begun to settle for less material or career fulfillment even though you may still long for more? Do you live, perhaps unconsciously, by the 25 percent rule—believing you "need 25 percent more money or status or achievement to feel successful" (p. 123)?

_____

_____

_____

3. If, like many of us, you still feel you haven't "arrived" in life, how are you coping with that? Are you trying to change occupations? Have you returned to school? Are you considering moving to another part of the country? Are you stewing inside? Have you thrown up your hands in despair? Have you stepped up the pace in your present situation, thinking if you can just do more you might be able to achieve your dreams? What are you doing to handle the disappointment?

_____

_____

_____

_____

_____

_____

4. In this chapter, Paula Rinehart suggests that we deal with our disappointment in at least two ways: (1) we change our "inner criteria by which we measure success" (p. 129), and (2) we delve to "the level of our deepest desires" to discover what we really want (p. 131). Take each of these suggestions and apply them to your situation. Do you see anything you might be able to change that will help you salvage some treasure from your broken dreams?

_____

_____

_____

_____

_____

_____

Chapter 10: An Honest Faith

1. Have you ever tied a dream to faith and had that dream dissipate before your eyes? If so, you know how difficult a loss that is. It strikes at the core of your understanding of God, your relationship to Him, His promises to you, and the nature and dependability of faith itself.

If you've ever lost such a dream, acknowledge that here. Describe the dream, how you thought God was wrapped up in it, how the dream was shattered, and what impact that had on your faith. Don't be afraid to be honest. God can handle your anger and hurt, as well as your fear.

_____

_____

_____

_____

_____

_____

_____

_____

_____

If this is the first time you have ever laid all this out and you have never taken it before God, or if you have prayed about this matter but still harbor some ill feelings over it, set aside some time to go to Him and tell Him all about it—no holds barred. As Paula Rinehart relates in this chapter, you'll find God longing to respond in a way that may very well surprise you by the level of its grace and mercy.

2. It's easy for us to put God in a box "where faithfulness or obedience on our part seems to obligate God to fulfill our desires" (p. 139). That is what Paula Rinehart calls a manageable belief system. It's not that beliefs about God are wrong but that once those beliefs belie the fact that God is personal and far more than we can ever imagine or comprehend, we end up with a God who isn't really God and a faith that isn't really biblical. True faith trusts without trying to control. False faith insists on the fulfillment of its own agenda. Which kind of faith was tied to your broken dreams? What kind of God had you embraced?

_____

_____

_____

_____

3. When our box around God collapses, we receive an opportunity to revise our understanding of God and embrace a faith that trusts open-endedly. But that can be confusing, disturbing, even frightening at first. What could help you through such a passage of faith?

In this chapter, Paula Rinehart mentions two factors that could come to your aid: (1) an honest heart, and (2) a willingness to let go of the familiar and accept uncertainty. These are not easy steps to take, but they're critical if you want to move on to a deeper relationship with the One who always works for your good.

Are you willing to take these steps? What can you do in the coming weeks that will put shoe leather on these steps of faith?

_____

_____

_____

_____

_____

Chapter 11: Saving the World

1. If you were a Christian during the '60s or early '70s, you know what an incredible emphasis was placed on reaching the world for Christ within a short time span. We were told, and we believed, that our generation would be the one to take the gospel to everyone worldwide. We were out to change the world, and there was no better way to do that than to win the world to Christ. But the mission went unfulfilled, and the world didn't change.

Of course, our generation expected to change the world in other ways too. We wanted to end racial prejudice, war, poverty, and injustice. We wanted to protect the environment and conquer space. We wanted so much, but we achieved so little—at least on the huge scale we had hoped.

Did you have any grandiose dreams? Have you ever been part of a much larger group trying to tackle an incredible problem? How did that make you feel? What kind of purpose did it give your life?

_____

_____

_____

_____

2. When the dream went unrealized, at least fully, how did you handle it? Did you simply abandon the dream and move on? Did you scale it down, making it more manageable to tackle? What did you do?

_____

_____

Can you identify with how Susan, Grant, Ted, or Paula handled their desire to change the world through focusing on their everyday experience (see pp. 150–51, 156–57)?

_____

_____

If you can recall, was such a shift in perspective disappointing? Did you feel as if you were settling for something much less desirable and worthwhile? Or did other feelings surface?

_____

_____

_____

3. Paula Rinehart suggests that when dreams become so big they become inherently unreachable it sets us up for disappointment. As she puts it, "Big is not just better—big is all that really matters. Those kinds of dreams have a disturbing tendency to backfire, for unless you can come up with a way to make sense of your small part, you are destined to be disappointed. When the big dream proves undoable, you are left asking if anyone else missed the train besides you. You are still wondering how to make your life count for something significant" (p. 152). Do you agree with this? Why or why not?

_____

_____

_____

_____

Do you still see yourself becoming trapped by the illusion that you can achieve the impossible? If so, how?

_____

_____

_____

4. Paula Rinehart points out several ways in which our generation has become skilled at creating change on a smaller scale. Below, each of those ways is listed. In the space provided, note which ones you've employed and how, and whether or not you find them satisfying.

We prefer to have a personal stake in the action.

_____

_____

We long for and seek to establish significant personal relationships.

_____

_____

We're not committed to the status quo; we like to challenge the norm.

_____

_____

We've developed patience in the process so that the journey, not just the arrival, has its own special significance.

_____

_____

We prefer a deeper experience of the genuine to the large and showy.

_____

_____

5. Paula Rinehart writes: "My craving for the momentous had almost spoiled me for being able to appreciate the joy in the ordinary. My attachment to big dreams had blinded me to those little, unpredictable, incandescent moments with people, when what is experienced is nothing less than the life of God in us and between us" (pp. 158–59). Can you relate to this? Could you be missing something special in the ordinary because of your disappointment in not achieving the extraordinary? Record your musings, then take them before God in prayer, asking Him to sensitize you to the incredible opportunities in the everyday happenings of your life.

_____

_____

_____

_____

_____

_____

Chapter 12: Fresh Starts

1. In the opening of this chapter, Paula Rinehart describes four paintings, each designed to depict a different stage in life. Of the four, which one best describes your current life stage?

_____

2. Because life is a process, it is full of transitions. We always seem to be moving from one stage to another. Paula Rinehart identifies three stages that commonly accompany transitions in life, especially midlife transitions. From what she says about them on pages 162–63, how would you describe each

stage, what's needed to go through each, and what could hinder one's passage through it? Use the chart below to record your answers.

TRANSITION STAGES

A BRIEF DESCRIPTION	NEEDS FOR PASSING THROUGH IT	HINDRANCES TO PASSAGE
(1)		
(2)		
(3)		

3. Paula Rinehart concludes the book by pointing out five more gifts—five precious treasures—found in the rubble of our disappointed dreams. Each of those is listed below. In the space provided, briefly describe each gift, then mention how, if at all, you can see each one present at the end of your own broken rainbows.

(1) The ability to ride looser in the saddle

What this means: _____

_____

How it gives grace to my life: _____

_____

_____

(2) Freer of illusions about life

What this means: _____

_____

How it gives grace to my life: _____

_____

_____

(3) The capacity to embrace life as it is

What this means: _____

_____

How it gives grace to my life: _____

_____

_____

(4) A quiet sense of gratitude

What this means: _____

_____

How it gives grace to my life: _____

_____

_____

(5) A realistic hope

What this means: _____

_____

How it gives grace to my life: _____

_____

_____

4. As you wrap up this study, take some time to record the most significant truths you learned about life, your generation, yourself, your relationships, and God. Then ask the Lord to help you recall and apply these truths as you continue on the journey called life.

TRUTHS I WANT TO REMEMBER

About life: _____

_____

_____

_____

_____

About my generation: _____

_____

_____

_____

_____

About myself: _____

_____

_____

_____

_____

About my relationships: _____

_____

_____

_____

_____

About God: _____

_____

_____

_____

_____

Notes

Chapter 1: An Invitation

1. Landon Jones, *Great Expectations: America and the Baby Boom Generation* (New York: Ballantine, 1980), 4.
2. John Dawson, *Taking Our Cities for God* (Lake City: Creation House, 1989), 92.

Chapter 2: Less Than We Bargained For

1. Dave Barry, *Dave Barry Turns 40* (New York: Crown, 1990), 2.
2. Cheryl Merser, *Grown-Ups: A Generation in Search of Adulthood* (New York: Putnam, 1987), 17.
3. Joan Harvey with Cynthia Katz, *The Imposter Phenomenon* (New York: Simon & Schuster, 1984).
4. Gail Sheehy, *Passages* (New York: Bantam, 1977), 376–412.
5. Paul C. Light, *Baby Boomers* (New York: Norton, 1988), 267.
6. Originally from the essay "The '60s Kids and the Crash" by P. J. O'Rourke, *The American Spectator* (February 1988), 16–17.

Chapter 3: The Children of Promise

1. From Morris Massey's video series, "You Are What You Were Then," which is a synopsis of generational distinctives.
2. Jones, *Great Expectations*, 283.
3. Lamentations 3:27, *New International Version*.
4. Jones, *Great Expectations*, 68.
5. Tom Matthews, "The Sixties Complex," *Newsweek*, 5 September 1988, 18.
6. Quoted from *Time*, 5 February 1965, in Jones, *Great Expectations*, 88.

Chapter 4: Broken Rainbows

1. The most commonly used series was Campus Crusade's "Ten Basic Steps to Christian Maturity," a helpful series of ten booklets on the basic aspects of the Christian life.
2. I am indebted to Paul Borthwick for this analogy.
3. William Bridges, *Transitions: Making Sense of Life's Changes* (Reading: Addison-Wesley, 1980), 37.
4. Bellah, *Baby Boom Believers*, 9.

Chapter 5: Rude Awakenings

1. Sue Monk Kidd, *When the Heart Waits* (San Francisco: Harper & Row, 1990), 84.
2. Daniel J. Levinson, *The Seasons of a Man's Life* (New York: Knopf, 1978), 71–126.
3. Theodore White, *In Search of History* (New York: Warner, 1978), 525.

Chapter 6: Inner Spaces

1. Gerald May, *Addiction and Grace* (San Francisco: Harper & Row, 1988), 102.
2. Quoted in Bridges, *Transitions*, 118.
3. John 1:42.
4. John 1:48.
5. Barry, *Dave Barry Turns 40*, 17.
6. Judith Viorst, *Necessary Losses* (New York: Ballantine, 1986), 299.
7. Randall Jarrell, quoted from *The New York Times*, 11 December 1983, in Viorst, *Necessary Losses*.

Chapter 7: Becoming Real

1. Larry Crabb, *Inside Out* (Colorado Springs: NavPress, 1988), 116–19.
2. 1 Peter 1:5.

Chapter 8: Loose Connections

1. Martin Seligman, "Boomer Blues," *Psychology Today*, October 1988, 52.
2. Viorst, *Necessary Losses*, 173.
3. See Dan Riley, *Living Together, Feeling Alone: Healing Your Hidden Loneliness* (New York: Prentice-Hall, 1989), for further explanation.

4. Sheehy, *Passages*, 358.
5. Bridges, *Transitions*, 58–70.
6. M. Scott Peck, *The Road Less Traveled* (New York: Simon & Schuster, 1978), 68.
7. Judith Viorst, "What Is This Thing Called Love?" *Reader's Digest*, August 1975, 65.

Chapter 9: Making It

1. Cheryl Russell, *100 Predictions for the Baby Boom* (New York: Plenium, 1987), 46.
2. Gilbert Grim, "Losing and Winning," *Psychology Today*, 52.
3. Merser, *Grown-Ups*, 130.
4. Douglas LaBier, *Modern Madness: The Emotional Fallout of Success* (Reading, Mass.: Addison-Wesley, 1987), 33.

Chapter 10: An Honest Faith

1. See Luke 15:31.
2. Jeremiah 20:7, *New American Standard Bible*.
3. May, *Addiction and Grace*, 107.

Chapter 11: Saving the World

1. Reprinted from "Act II, Scene ii" in *The Weather of the Heart*, by Madeleine L'Engle @ 1978 by Crosswicks. Used by permission of Harold Shaw Publishers, Wheaton, Ill.

Chapter 12: Fresh Starts

1. Bridges, *Transitions*, 28–52.
2. Ibid., 136.
3. Madeleine L'Engle, *The Summer of the Great Grandmother* (San Francisco: Harper & Row, 1974), 180.
4. Levinson, *Seasons*, 29.
5. Garrison Keillor, *Lake Wobegon Days* (New York: Viking Penguin, 1985), 337.
6. C. S. Lewis, *The Problem of Pain* (New York: Macmillan, 1962), 115.

Moody Press, a ministry of the Moody Bible Institute,
is designed for education, evangelization, and edification.
If we may assist you in knowing more about Christ
and the Christian life, please write us without obligation:
Moody Press, c/o MLM, Chicago, Illinois 60610.